Colors On My Canvas

Colors On My Canvas

César E. Becerra

authorHOUSE®

AuthorHouse™
1663 Liberty Drive
Bloomington, IN 47403
www.authorhouse.com
Phone: 1-800-839-8640

Published by AuthorHouse   02/10/2012

ISBN: 978-1-4685-5077-1 (sc)
ISBN: 978-1-4685-5097-9 (e)

Library of Congress Control Number: 2012902154

Contents

Dedication: This work is dedicated to all the people that make up my heart and have made me who I am, to my wonderful and supporting wife who I credit with challenging me to express my emotions, my seeds for allowing me to understand my purpose in life, my parents who have been my first and most important teachers, and to everyone who has the courage and introspection to understand that change in the world begins with change in yourself.

Colors On My Canvas is a collection of writing accumulated throughout the years based on the wonderful stories and lessons learned through the hearts and souls of people I have come in contact with. The attempt with this work was to create a picture that was nowhere near perfect yet accurate regarding the realities of the world that we live in and the people that we share it with. The colors on my canvas have shaped and influenced everything about me. They are my reality and by extension our reality. The search for identity has been a long and painful struggle throughout my life and it is a journey that I will be on until my final breath is taken and my final words are spoken. Just like I am many things to different people you carry with you many layers of identity that collectively make up the unique individual that you are. Understanding who you are is the first step in creating your path and destiny. The collection of photographs in this work is very special to me because it reminds me of a lesson I have learned from my experience on my journey through this world. Art does not have to imitate life to be real and life does not have to imitate art to be false. Art IS life and life IS art when we capture the right moments in time without even knowing someone is watching. In closing, this work is a revealing look at my hopes, fears, regrets, wishes and dreams and it is recognition of the importance of every person that has made an impact in my life. It is through their love, inspiration, courage and success that I find peace and happiness in my own life. My philosophy in life is to give more than you take. I hope that when my time on this earth ends it is because I had nothing more to give.

Respectfully,

César E. Becerra

"To the world you are just one person; to one person you might be the

world." Unknown

¡Mexika Tiahui!

Chapter 1

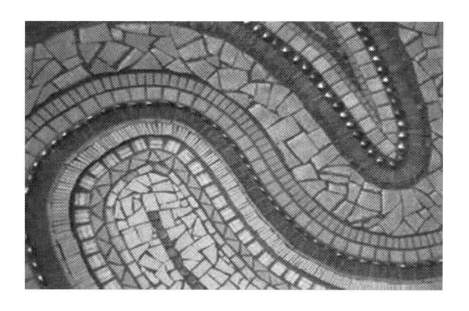

First Words

My Mission

The mission of my life is to mold leaders with my passion;

Mold children into warriors and turn inspiration into action.

I will be a searcher of lost souls like the one that in me I found;

I will let the world hear me without even making a sound.

I am not the words that I speak, I am the things you see me do.

I am not the one who thinks youth have potential I am the one who always knew.

I will capture every opportunity to help them all believe;

They can do much more with their lives than what others think they can achieve.

Judge me from the beginning to the end, like a good film or a great book;

I am a person who spent their life looking to give before they took.

I am not the one who worries about the certainty of death;

I have decided to live every moment and appreciate every breath.

I will let my passion guide me, eternally searching for the truth;

My life will be sacrificed for tomorrow and a better future for our youth.

I don't have to be who you want me to be; I know how to succeed;

I don't have to be anyone I am not, I'm not afraid to just be me.

Life is so short and goes so quickly, you will be judged by what you leave;

I hope to leave behind hope and empathy in the form of growing seeds.

I will accept the things I cannot change, yet I won't be afraid to cry;

And the things that I can change: I will find the courage in me to try.

I will live my life as a visionary in hopes that one day the blind will see;

I will continue fighting the battles until the day my heart is free.

I am . . .

I am Cesar.

I am humble and proud.

I wonder how my life will end.

I hear rain inside my mind.

I see peace in the world.

I want to be the best person I can.

I am humble and proud.

I pretend to be fearless.

I feel time moving too fast.

I touch my heart to feel its beat.

I worry about not reaching my dream.

I cry when I realize there are things I cannot change.

I am humble and proud.

I understand that joy and pain are part of living.

I say I am in control.

I dream about rising together.

I try to give as much as I can.

I hope the future will be bright.

I am humble and proud.

I am Cesar.

César E. Becerra

A new life awaits me

My Prayer

Creator:

Thank you for the gift of life that you have given me and for giving me everything that I have ever truly needed. Thank you for the opportunity to experience a healthy body and a creative mind and for living inside me with your unconditional love, your pure and boundless spirit, and your warm and radiant light. Thank you for using my words, eyes, and heart to share your love wherever I go. I love you although I don't know who or what you are, and because I am your creation, I love myself just the way I am. Help me keep the peace and passion in my heart and to have the courage to be the person you need me to be. Please grant me the humility to recognize my mistakes and the compassion to make amends for them. Give me the will to choose right over wrong and the capacity to accept people for who they are. I will forever be grateful for your ability to forgive and believe in me despite my many flaws. Help me to mirror your image in mortal form and to echo your words through my actions. I implore you to guide me in the direction of your voice and to never desert me. I will be strong because of you. I will live my life in love because you always love me.

Amén.

Nunca Sabes Lo Que Tienes

Tanta belleza en este mundo que día con día es ignorada.

Tanto queremos obtener y nos olvidamos que tal vez no habrá mañana.

Yo caí victima a esa trampa de vivir mi vida aprisa;

Pocas veces paré a contemplar el aroma de una flor o el valor de una sonrisa.

Por vivir mi vida rápido así fue que se acabó;

¿Hoy me pregunto si fui yo o nuestro padre quien me la quito?

Él nunca me dio mi vida, él solo me la presto;

Yo sí tuve una oportunidad, y fui yo quien la desperdició.

Pude hacer yo tantas cosas; remediar algún error.

¿Por qué ignoraba mi consciencia? ¿Por qué le temía al amor?

Tantas preguntas sin respuesta que se han perdido en el viento;

Viví toda mi vida en hambre y nunca encontré el alimento.

Nos quejamos de tantas cosas y nos ciega a la verdad.

¿Tenemos tanto que no apreciamos, porque nos damos a la vanidad?

Muchas lecciones solo se aprenden cuando el remedio ya no existe;

Esta es una de esos ejemplos porque de mi tú ya te fuiste.

Espero que alguien aprenda de mis errores ya que yo siempre tuve miedo;

Nunca sabes lo que tienes hasta que tu alma sube al cielo.

En ese instante, todo cambia y nunca sabrás lo que te espera;

Ya no controlas tu destino, de tu cuerpo nada queda.

Lo que queda en el mundo es la herencia que dejaste;

¿Cuánto amor plantaste en semillas? ¿Cuánto fruto cosechaste?

Te suplico por favor que no gastes tu vida buscando un tesoro;

Ese tesoro ya lo tienes . . . tener la vida es tenerlo todo.

Sunrise in paradise just a few days
after marriage

Smile

How much does a smile cost?

Nothing . . . . So smile!

How much is a smile worth?

You never know; and this is why you smile.

A smile can change your day. Just one day can change your life.

César E. Becerra

SONRISA ETERNA

Tú eres la alegría de mis ojos

Que brillan más que nunca con amor.

Me miro en el espejo y veo en mi rostro

Lo mucho que ha cambiado quien yo soy.

Memorias tan hermosas que hoy yo tengo

Y siempre estoy pensando en tu mañana.

Te juro que hare todo de mi parte

Para que seas quien tú puedes ser.

Como quisiera, que tú me vieras,

Que tú sonrisa jamás se apague

Y mi alegría, sea tuya siempre.

Sonrisa eterna; Mi mayor anhelo;

Con cada día le doy las gracias

Por su regalo . . . . Tú vida.

La La La La La La La La La La La La Lalala aaaa

Yo he cambiado desde que llegaste,

Desde ese día hasta hoy ya se vivir.

Y aunque tengo prestada mi existencia

Se lo mucho que yo quiero hacer por ti.

De obscura soledad tú me salvaste;

Hoy esa soledad es Gran Orgullo.

Nunca dudes quien eres en mi vida

Mi corazón y amor es siempre tuyo.

Como quisiera, que tú me vieras,

Que tú sonrisa jamás se apague

Y mi alegría, sea tuya siempre.

Sonrisa eterna; Mi mayor anhelo;

Con cada día le doy las gracias

Por su regalo . . . . Tu vida.

La La La La La La La La La La La La Lalala aaaa

Sonrisa Eterna . . . .

La La La La La La La La La La La La Lalala aaaa

Sonrisa Eterna, Eterna . . . .

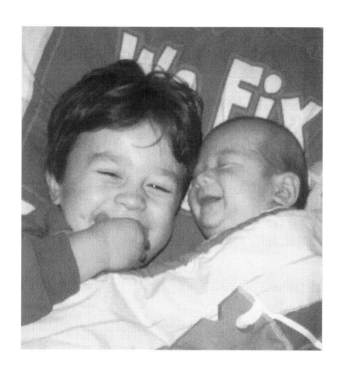

Sus eternas sonrisas son mi razón para vivir

Chapter 2

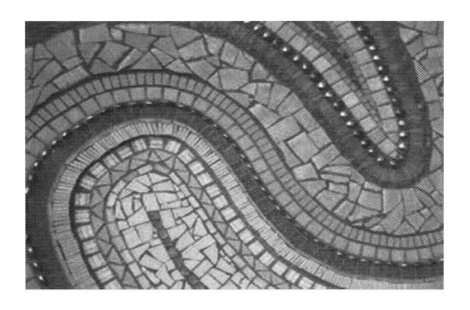

Hoy Comprendo

Has Sido Bueno Conmigo

Cuando pienso en el pasado
Y analizo mi presente;
Me doy cuenta de lo que te debo,
Por lo que has hecho ciegamente.

Has confiado en mí tantas veces
Cuando quizás no lo merecía;
Me alumbrabas el camino
Cuando ocupaba una guía.

Todo a cambio de nada
Solo esperanza de que algún día,
Logrará yo conocerte
Y cambiara yo mi vida.

Y aun así yo me quejaba
Pensando que nunca escuchaste.
Pero fui yo quien te ignoraba,
Y buscaba amor en otra parte.

No podía ver claramente
Y caminaba en la neblina;
Solo hay un lugar
Donde hay amor puro y sin medida.

Hoy me siento afortunado
Por la vida que me has dado;
Reconozco mi oportunidad
De hacer el bien a tu lado.

Espero algún día me perdones
Por durar tanto tiempo en tocar la puerta;
No tenía la valentía
Hoy me has dado tú la fuerza.

Y aun con todos mis errores
Has sido bueno conmigo;
Mi pregunta sin respuesta es:
¿Por qué razón siempre te olvido?

César E. Becerra

*The quest for true spirituality
is an eternal journey*

Only You

I don't have the eyes to see you
And I don't have the courage to find you.
I don't have strength to continue
Or the voice I need to call you.
I have gone through this many times before
Peaks and valleys have been my life.
Some way or another I have survived
After the dark soon comes the light.
I have tried to follow you on many days
But don't know how to steer a straight path.
Surrounded daily with temptation
And I am merely another man.
A man who was born to be a sinner
That's the truth although hard to believe.
That is the reason that you died for us
Yet we still want more than we need.
I am tired of disappointing you
Or perhaps I can't meet my expectations.
I know that you will always love me
Despite my flaws, I'm your creation.
Please help me understand
That there are things I cannot change.
Please teach me what you want me to learn,
Please allow me to be brave.
I have asked so many questions
About things I often ponder,
Yet no one has ever listened,
It's only you who has the answers.

Me Salvaste

Me salvaste el día en que nací aunque no te lo pedí.

Y cuando no podía yo llorar, me enseñaste a sentir.

Vivía ciego y sin esperanza y me enseñaste a creer.

No confiaba en mi talento y me ayudaste a poder ver.

Las veces que quise yo dejarte me mostraste tu gran amor.

Y cuando estaba por los suelos tú aliviaste mi dolor.

Me salvaste cuando sin pensar iba a traicionar yo mi mente.

Me enseñaste que para triunfar tenía que ayudar a nuestra gente.

No sé cómo agradecerte por todo lo que me has dado.

Me enseñaste a perdonar y a no vivir en el pasado.

Sabes, tú me has hecho fuerte porque me enseñaste con acciones

Lo que en palabras y en retratos no se aprenden las lecciones.

Cuando cumpla yo mi meta, y llegue yo contigo,

Te pediré que me disculpes, mi salvador, mi gran amigo.

Hoy Comprendo . . .

Hoy comprendo finalmente que unas cosas no son lo que parecen.

También entiendo que mi alegría viene junta con la de mi gente.

Hoy comprendo que hay preguntas que no tienen una respuesta.

Y que hay que siempre ser optimistas y cultivar la paciencia.

Hoy comprendo mi existencia y el poder de la esperanza.

Tantos años la buscaba y la cargaba en el alma.

Tantas cosas que hoy comprendo, ¿porque no pude entender ayer?

Quizás esa sea una de esas preguntas, "¿Cómo puedes creer sin ver?"

Hoy comprendo que eres ciego si nunca abres tu corazón.

Lo verdaderamente importante no se ve con ojos y tiene infinito valor.

Lo más bello no apreciamos aunque casi siempre es gratis;

Son las cosas que ignoramos y olvidamos demasiado fácil.

Tantas cosas intentabas enseñarme y no escuché.

Cuanto daría por regresar el tiempo pero mi tiempo ya se fue.

Hoy comprendo que nunca me abandonaste aunque siempre lo pensé.

Eternamente me arrepiento, fui yo quien te dejé.

César E. Becerra

Why Not?

Why try to be positive when everything around you seems so negative?

Why try to improve the future when chances are that you won't get to see it?

Why fight for social justice if it's a battle we can't win?

Why try to create smiles when our face is full of tears?

Why try to make the changes needed to improve our lives?

Why try to make a difference? Is it worth the trouble to fight?

Why try to light a candle to get your mind out of the dark?

Why try inspiring youth when it seems like it won't help?

Why try to be the spark that lights the fire against injustice?

Why try to live in empathy where apathy is the common practice?

I don't have the answers to many questions but the ones above have a simple answer. People have asked me all of my life and I have replied with that simple answer: Those aren't the questions we should be asking; the real question is just one: Instead of always asking why, how about once, asking **why not?**

Aprende a Valorar

¿Porque no sabemos valorar las cosas que tenemos?

Tenemos más que suficiente pero nunca lo entendemos.

¿Cuándo te quejas de tus penas porque no te pones a pensar?

Por más grande que sea tu apuro, alguien tiene muchos más.

Yo caí en esa trampa de desear lo que no tengo,

Pero gracias al destino, cambie mi vida justo a tiempo.

Hoy aprecio tantas cosas que mucho antes ignore;

Comprendo que las cosas más simples también se pueden perder.

¿Cuantas veces has dado gracias, solamente por tener la vida?

¿Cuándo satisfaces tu hambre, das gracias por el pan del día?

Son las cosas más sencillas las que nunca valoramos;

Estamos tan perdidos, y su nombre no llamamos.

El regalo de ser padre deja un fruto sin medida;

Para tus hijos lo eres todo y ellos son tu alegría.

Con mucho orgullo le das tu abrazo y como brillan las sonrisas;

Consumen toda tu mente y como aprecian tus caricias.

Las sencillas caricias tienen valor, de esto yo te aseguro;

No tienes que ir muy lejos, pregúntale a alguien que no las tuvo.

Aprende a valorar lo que realmente es importante;

Aprécialo hoy, quizás mañana será muy tarde.

A breathtaking view just after sunset

Preguntas Sin Respuesta

¿Por qué existe gente que disfruta humillar a los demás?

¿Por qué prefiere uno mentir aun estando en frente de la verdad?

¿Cuál fue el día en que tome mi primer paso en alejarme?

Me siento tan distante y no he podido relajarme.

Mi mente está llena de pensamientos y preguntas sin respuesta.

Es difícil dormir tranquilo y estar despierto me molesta.

¿Cuando decidí callar y no expresar lo que yo siento?

¿Qué día me resigne y le regale mi sueño al viento?

¿Cuándo te conoceré, para hablarte cara a cara?

¿Y al llegar el último día podré seguir en mi jornada?

He vivido mucho tiempo sin entender mi lugar en el mundo;

Estoy consciente que mi vida es prestada, y que tu amor es muy profundo.

Te pido un último regalo después de tantos que me has dado;

Dame el valor para quererte igual como tú me has amado.

Hasta ese día seguiré perdido, caminando en la neblina;

Ayúdame a ser quien tú has deseado, dale un propósito a mi vida.

Seguiré mi vida preguntando, tal vez algún día cambiare;

Quizás el día que te conozca finalmente entenderé.

*Muchas preguntas encuentran respuestas
cuando descubres tus raíces*

One Last Question

Today I made a decision, my life changes from now on.
I will not pretend to smile I can no longer hide my frown.
I will consume myself with passion; I'll let it blind me from the light;
I don't want to be an actor; I want to believe our future is bright.

In the past I tried to make some changes, but they have never seemed enough;
My vision and aspirations have not gotten me very far.
In my mind I wasn't successful because the goal was never small,
Perhaps I set myself up for failure, perhaps I was the one who caused my fall.

I'm more confused now than ever, I see roads in all directions;
My heart can't help me this time, and my soul seeks inspiration.
Should I continue on just living, walking a path I'm not sure is mine?
Or should I end my fight forever, and hope a dream I'll one day find?

As you can see I'm at the crossroads, I have no clue which way to go;
If I knew where each one led to, I'd pick the one that helps us grow.
One last question remains inside me, and the answer has not come;
I am tired now and weakened, I don't like the person I've become.

Right now I don't feel sure of anything; my life has lost the motivation;
I feel like I'm walking alone aimlessly with all my pain and no sedation.
I have never felt this feeling; I've always perceived myself as strong,
Perhaps I was mistaken; perhaps i have been wrong all along.

I leave my fate at your discretion; I am no longer in control;
You can decide which way to take me, you can write my final song.
From today on I'm a follower; I give you full control of my heart,
You have the freedom now to guide me, although you've done that from the start.

I felt I understood the world but in fact I knew much less than I thought.
I learned from experience, my mistakes, and all the battles that I fought.
I have learned that my life was different; I have learned that my struggle was tough;
But I could never answer my last question . . . . why was my best just not enough?

Chapter 3

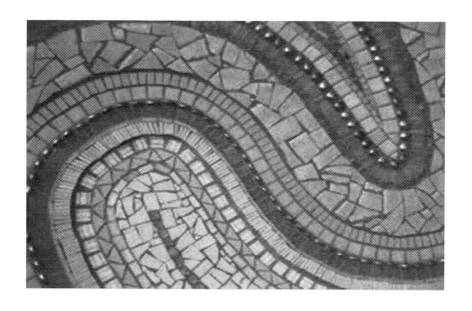

El Día Que Renací

La vida es dura y tal vez injusta;

Esto lo llevo siempre en mente.

Nada en la vida es prometido,

Seguiré luchando por mi gente.

In Case I Never Learn to Fly:
To my future child:

In case I never learn to fly, please remember that every moment was special;
The satisfaction comes in the journey and the memories that we treasure.

There is no shame in trying and failing unless you compromise yourself;
I failed many times on many days but I never ignored my heart.

I can't go back to when I was younger, yet I don't live with any regrets;
Mistakes are part of living; you must strive to be YOUR best.

Maybe my best just wasn't good enough for I was never satisfied.
It's a difficult way to be happy but you must always try to aim high.

I did that all of my life, perhaps I never gave myself a chance;
But I felt if I did not believe in me, why would anybody else?

I hope you forgive me for not being who I could have been or who I was;
Just know that I always loved you although my time with you is lost.

One more thing I have to tell you in case I never learn to fly;
I was thinking of tomorrow, it was for you that I always tried.

My only regret is not being with you if my dreams should go astray;
I will forever smile down on you . . . . I hope your tomorrow is a better day.

Estas Palabras

Estas palabras que yo escribo
Te las regalo humildemente;
Tantas cosas que me has dado
Es un sueño hoy tenerte.

Estas palabras no son mías,
Viajan de mi corazón al tuyo;
Desde el día que tú llegaste
Has sido mi más grande orgullo.

Cada sonrisa es mi alegría.
Cada mirada es inspiración.
Cada partida es tristeza.
Cada llanto es mi dolor.

Me has enseñado a apreciar la vida
Ya ver lo que no había jamás visto.
Has cambiado mi manera de pensar;
Para ser padre nunca estás listo.

Tener tu amor es algo bello,
Ayer fuiste solo una ilusión.
Hoy sin ti yo no soy nada,
Eres la música en mi canción.

Una promesa sí te hago
Porque de algo estoy seguro;
Mientras el señor me de la fuerza,
Lucharé cada día por tu futuro.

No sé qué hice para merecerte;
Cada día es memorable.
Hoy sin duda soy completo;
Espero nunca defraudarte.

Estas palabras que yo escribo
Te las regalo humildemente;
Tengo nueva razón para vivir,
Doy gracias a Dios por conocerte.

Por Si Algún Día te Preguntan

Tú llegada cambio mi vida,

Te lo he dicho muchas veces,

Tanto tiempo sin saber mi propósito.

Con cada logro tuyo mi orgullo crece.

Ha pasado tanto tiempo,

Aún recuerdo esa mañana.

Habia perdido la esperanza,

Tú me ayudaste a encontrarla.

No entendia lo que tenia,

Tú me ayudaste a verlo claro.

Tenia todo lo que necesitaba

Tenia que dejar atrás el pasado.

Fuiste una bendición del cielo,

Cada dia me siento más afortunado.

Solo una sonrisa tuya

Convierte mi invierno a un verano.

Aunque aún eres pequeño

Explicaré el origen de tu nombre.

Escoger tu nombre no fue fácil,

Quiero que sepas como y donde.

Cada letra de tu nombre

La escribi en un papel;

En mi mente solo una meta:

Captar lo que tú llegaste a ser.

Pensamos en una frase

Que representara lo que eras;

Dos vinieron a mi mente,

O quizás solo fueron las primeras.

El Señor Ama Infinitamente,

Cada dia lo compruebo.

El Sueño Ayer Imaginado,

Cada sonrisa me hace nuevo.

Should the rain decide to leave me,

Or should it decide to stay;

I have to welcome each opportunity

I have to value every day.

De regreso a la misión

El Sueño Más Grande

Muchos dicen que la vida no es vida sin soñar;

Yo fui soñador por mucho tiempo y vi a varios sueños fracasar.

En la vida siempre hay excusas y si las buscas las encuentras;

La persona que no le teme al fracaso no necesita tomar cuentas.

Antes de triunfar por ley aun no escrita tendrás que fracasar;

Como reaccionas al fracaso es lo que hará tus sueños realidad.

Mis sueños siempre han sido humildes, yo siempre quise ayudar;

Nuestra gente necesita inspiración y pocos la quieren regalar.

Mi vida cambió por completo el día que tú llegaste a mí,

Te he dicho antes y hoy te repito, fue el día que renací.

Desde ese día era un hombre nuevo y mi pasado no importaba;

Disfrutaba del presente, y miré el futuro en tu mirada.

Hoy mi sueño lo llevo por dentro y solo tú y yo sabremos,

Si mi sueño se realiza; con el tiempo lo veremos.

Quisiera estar siempre contigo; aliviar tu sed y quitarte el hambre;

El sueño más grande de mi vida es algún día ser buen padre.

One of those special moments captured in time

Un Solo Día

Hoy fue un solo día, pero aun tan diferente;

Empezó como cualquier otro, pero lo llevaré siempre en mi mente.

Despertaste al amanecer porque sentías la cama fría;

Viniste a donde estábamos con tu linda mirada de alegría.

Te preparé tu cepillo de dientes y cepillamos lado a lado;

Sin saber que este día más que otros dejabas atrás el pasado.

Te ayudé a cambiar tu ropa; un par de "shorts" y una camisa;

La camisa era de Mickey, y me gané una sonrisa.

Logre ponerte calcetines, aunque tú no los querías;

Te puse tus zapatos nuevos, encaprichado todavía.

Tomaste leche con galletas, para tener más energía;

Hay que ponerle algo al estómago al inicio de cada día.

Se acercaba la salida, te puse un abrigo porque hacia frio;

Peiné tu cabello con mis manos y comenzamos el camino.

Al llegar a nuestro destino salimos juntos mano en mano;

Te encaminé hacía la puerta y me agache hacía tu lado.

Te regalé un fuerte abrazo y un tierno beso esa mañana;

Te puse tu mochila, mire tus ojos, y de repente sonó la campana.

Hoy será un solo día pero lo llevaré siempre en mi mente;

Tu primer día de escuela; no puedo expresar lo que se siente.

11/9/10

Listo para conocer el mundo

Why I tried

I understood my limitations and that often people want to see you fall;
For me nothing ever came easy, every blessing, every challenge, I was grateful for it all.
Life is not about the beginning or even the final destination;
Life is all about the journey and the search for inspiration.
That eternal search for me ended the first time I looked into your eyes;
From that moment I was a new person . . . . ready to make any sacrifice.
It is hard to change your ways when you are content with how you are living;
It is hard to keep a positive mind when your heart has stopped believing.
I want to be a better person so you can grow up to be strong;
I don't want you to come as far as I have; my dream is for you to go beyond.
Many successes and many failures it's almost foolish to keep track;
Failure must come before success; just keep going and don't look back.
Any positive contribution that you can make to society is so important;
I want to give hope for the future even if it is only in small doses.
All my dreams and all my wishes I might never get to achieve;
I won't let my fears control me, goals in life are meant to be reached.
Every day is an opportunity; I will embrace the possibility.
I will search my soul for courage and live my life in true humility.
My life will have a purpose, now my task is to pursue it;
I have identified the occasion, now . . . . I must rise to it.
"Some things will never change", I have heard it all my life;
If you ever wonder about me . . . . you are the reason why I tried.

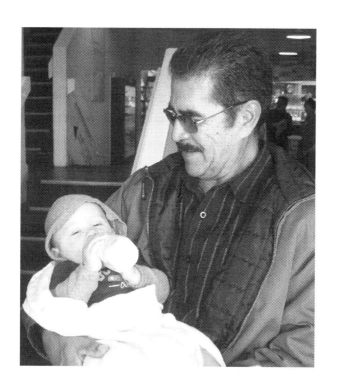

Those last few seconds before a nap

El Día Que Renací

Por: Un Alma Moribunda

Algún día fui moribundo en mi alma y corazón;
Era una piedra vagabunda, sin esperanza y buscando amor.

No encontraba lo que buscaba porque no tenía fe en mí;
Simplemente renegaba por cada día que me perdí.

No sentía que estaba vivo, era la sombra de un fantasma;
Por afuera lo escondía, pero por dentro no había calma.

Cometí muchos errores pero de cada uno aprendí;
En la vida siempre hay tropiezos . . . adelante hay que seguir.

La experiencia fue mí maestra y aprendí varias lecciones;
Levantar en cada caída y sembrar amor en corazones.

Pero la pregunta más vieja cada noche me espantaba;
"¿Será posible vivir realmente sin entender que Dios me amaba?"

Un segundo día de agosto de un año aprendí;
Mi razón para vivir tenía nombre, ese nombre fue Esai.

Hijo, eras El Sueño Ayer Imaginado que más te puedo decir;
Llegaste tú y en un instante me enseñaste a vivir.

El Señor Ama Infinitamente; tu vida lo comprobó;
El día que naciste encontré mi alma . . . fue el mismo día que renació.

Un sueño se convierte en realidad

Con Dinero o Sin Dinero

"Con dinero o sin dinero",

Dice una clásica canción.

Con dinero o sin dinero,

Sigue viva mi pasión.

En la vida valoramos a

Lo que tiene un alto precio;

Y a veces confundimos

El don de vida por un derecho.

Cada día es un regalo,

Con el tiempo comprobé.

Lo olvidé por un momento,

Y un día de enero me acordé.

El éxito más grande hasta

Este punto de mi vida,

Fue traer a un ser al mundo

Que en mí, buscara sabiduría.

Tengo tanto que enseñarle,

Y el tiempo es prestado.

Cada día es una oportunidad,

¿Y cuántos la han desperdiciado?

Con dinero o sin dinero,

Hoy tengo mi tesoro.

Con dinero o sin dinero . . . .

Yo ya lo tengo todo.

The day our little jaguar warrior came to us

The Meaning Behind Your Name

The day we found out you were coming was a very special day;

The sun shone a little brighter than the typical day in May.

We were blessed with your older brother and now we were being blessed again;

The feeling was amazing and much too difficult to explain.

Unlike the first time, we decided that we would find out your gender before your birth;

After 3 long months of speculation, one afternoon we finally knew.

By chance it happened to be August 30th, the day that brought your father to the world;

The news was a revelation that brought a myriad of emotion; my one treasure would now be plural.

I forgot it was my birthday because I was so wrapped up in the power of the moment;

Another boy, a burning fire, a flowing river, another warrior to fight the torrent.

From that day forward I became obsessed with searching for and finding you the perfect name,

Perhaps not perfect to society, or anyone who didn't know what "struggle" meant.

The first name had to be graceful, portray your spirit and be unique;

It had to be a symbol of strength, courage, and of eternal will to succeed.

You were named after the jaguar, an animal of great significance for indigenous cultures;

The animal had the traits that we will teach you that will mold you into a warrior.

The jaguar warriors were the fighters and the defenders of their people;

The jaguar conveys power and an image that is equally fierce as it is regal.

You were conceived in the same year as the centennial celebration of the Mexican revolution;

At that time people were tired of blatant injustice, they felt voiceless and were lacking a solution.

Our ancestors decided to rise up against corruption, come together, and fight the wrong;

They sought their own inner warrior; looked inside their soul and found the courage to be strong.

That struggle brought many leaders and heroes, many of them gave up their life;

Of all those courageous leaders, martyrs, and legends one in particular came to mind.

El General Zapata was a man of vision, of unimpressive stature, but great heart;

He led the fight for what people starved for: the elusive justice, land, and "libertad".

His first name was Emiliano; your middle name will be his tribute;

Don't worry about people pronouncing it, just make sure that they can feel you.

The meaning behind your name is as complex as is your charge;

I promise to do my best to get you ready; then it will be my great joy to watch.

You have an opportunity many take for granted; to live and make a difference;

In this eternal fight for justice . . . . Don't be afraid to go the distance.

For My Son: Nahuel Milian

You carry the courage of the jaguar and the spirit of revolution.

Trust the struggle in your heart and be a part of the solution.

Con Una Tierna Mirada

Con el tiempo vas cambiando y el mundo es diferente;

Los amigos con los que creciste se van, y los reemplaza nueva gente.

Antes para todo había tiempo pero hoy reconoces que cada día es

prestado;

El mañana no es seguro y no se puede hacer nada en el pasado.

La vida es más lenta pero rápidamente los días se van;

Te enseñan a apreciar lo simple y a distinguir las batallas que hay

que pelear.

En el mundo hay pocas cosas que defenderías con tu vida;

Sin pensarlo, en un instante, por ello todo lo darías.

Cada sonrisa es inolvidable, cada abrazo es calor;

Cada logro es mí orgullo, cada fracaso es mi dolor.

Me han enseñado a ser hombre, y no por simplemente ser su padre;

Hoy soy hombre por tener la valentía de luchar para formar un hogar

estable.

Aprovecharé cada día porque mañana es muy tarde;

La meta será noble: Que mi cariño nunca les falte.

Ustedes son mi todo, son mi luz, son mi alegría;

Con una tierna mirada, le dan aliento a mi ser y cada día me motivan.

My boys catching a break from the Arizona summer heat

Como Agua Entre Mis Manos

El día que tú naciste me diste una oportunidad;

Una oportunidad que agradezco a diario

En un instante cambiaste mi realidad.

Ya no era quien fui antes, era diferente por completo;

Hoy y siempre serás mi orgullo,

Cuanto te adoro nunca será secreto.

Poco a poco conocerás el mundo y las leyes de la vida;

Sin duda me harás muchas preguntas,

Espero contestarlas con paciencia y sabiduría.

Pero pronto llegará el día cuando no tendré una respuesta;

Espero tener el valor para decírtelo

Y así lograré poner una muestra.

Creemos saber mucho de este mundo,

Pero hay mucho más que no sabemos;

Sigue fielmente al corazón y sin duda encontraras tu rumbo.

En la vida sabemos poco, es mejor reconocerlo;v

La sed del conocimiento y la alegría

Hará que aproveches de tu tiempo.

El tiempo para el hombre no es eterno y algún día te dejaré;

Sin embargo recuerda siempre,

Que nunca y por nada te olvidaré.

Que pronto corre la vida, un día llegas y para el otro nos vamos;

Como agua entre mis manos . . . .

Así se van los años.

*Un lindo atardecer en California y
pronto vendrá un humilde amanecer*

Tal vez Mañana no Vendrá

Aprecia todo en esta vida porque cada día es un regalo;

Cada sonrisa, y caricia, cada abrazo de un hermano.

Tantas cosas he aprendido, hoy soy un hombre con valor;

Hoy me enfrento a mis temores, hoy no escondo mi dolor.

Mi dolor es no ser todo lo que para ti yo quise ser;

Mi dolor es no tener el tiempo para enseñarte lo que se.

Hoy no tomo nada en vano, y mi vida tiene significado;

Yo seré eternamente feliz mientras te tenga a ti a mi lado.

Cuando te olvidas de la ley eterna que algún día moriremos;

Es como tener una respuesta en plena vista y sin embargo no la vemos.

Esperaré pacientemente, algún día el cambio a mi alma llegará;

El ayer hoy ya no existe y tal vez mañana no vendrá.

Padre e hijo en el lugar donde
inicio nuestra familia

Chapter 4

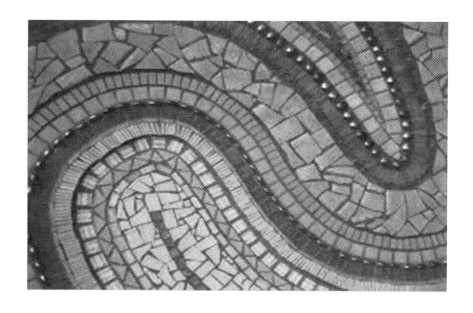

The Measure of a Man

Dreamer

All my life I've been a dreamer and tried to fight to change the wrong. I have struggled with my choices because I feel a pressure to be strong. How can I be weak and fragile when my makers define courage? How can I give in to challenges when my ancestors lived right through them? I will always be optimistic and believe in my abilities but the hardest thing for me to accept is apathy and a lack of feeling. That's a poison we must battle if we are to have hope for our survival, we need to start to seek solutions instead of being stuck on all the problems. Those solutions, we'll reach collectively if we are working hand in hand; together we are much stronger than the strength of just one man. I accept my responsibilities and understand my limitations; I can't create change on my own but I can influence generations. I consider myself a teacher, in every sense of the word; teaching is an act of love, although at times we go unheard. It's those times that you feel no one listens when perhaps something gets through, slowly you help change the future in ways you thought you never could. I will continue being a dreamer although at times it seems too late; what I hope is that I don't give up dreaming and that from my dream I never wake.

César E. Becerra

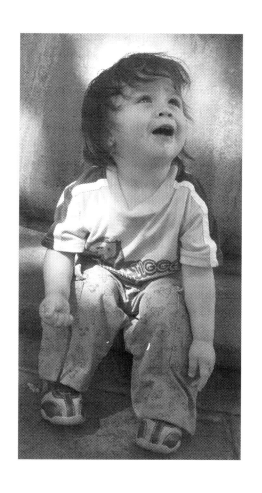

My oldest son Esai staring up into the sky

Imagine

Imagine being judged by what is inside of you and not feeling second rate;
How about walking alone at night, being female and not worrying about being
raped? A simple cruise through your neighborhood and seeing no gang tags on
the walls. Turning on the news at night and hearing no negative news at all.
A school where kids seek learning, not just for the last bell to sound; a child
that grows with inner confidence and is not always being put down.

Imagine a country that is free, in real actions not just in words.
How about following the constitution instead of using it to exclude? You still
say that we are equal, you aren't just crazy; you are blind too. And what if
our history took a left turn and you never took our land? What if you became
the outsider? How much hate could you withstand? What makes one person
in this country better than the next man? Do you know what borders really
are? They are just lines written in sand.

Imagine life with no rushing, when you could always take your time. What's
the point of accumulating material wealth when you never have a clear mind?
Why do we live our lives in apathy always looking the other way? Look at
that street corner, what do that beggar's eyes convey? This country uses people
when they need them, sucks them dry then spits them out. Is not that what
happens? Sometimes I feel a need to shout. We must seek to find solutions,
we must seek to organize, we are talking about our future; don't you think
it's worth a try?

Imagine bringing children in to this world knowing they'll have a place to play.
Better yet, let us think of their future, do you think that they'll be safe? What
do they have to look forward to besides the pain we left behind? They have no
option in the matter; they don't choose to be alive. I am afraid to bring a child
where ignorance and greed reign supreme. How could I stay positive when all of
this is just MY dream? This is not our world to ruin, we are merely passing by. I
wonder when we'll see this; I wonder who will hear my cry . . . Imagine.

My youngest son Nahuel looking
over a wall to catch a view

Homeward Bound

I am lost in a distant place,
Is a dream I often have.

People there greet me with smiles,
Yet I can't figure why I'm sad.

I set my sights on a bright future,
But I have done that all along.

I have goals I must achieve.
I know through it all I must be
strong.

It's always raining in my mind,
Though outside it never rains.

My mind has no time for resting,
It's consumed with all the strain.

The strain of a cold world
And of a past now left behind.

Although on the outside I smile,
Deep inside my soul quietly cries.

It cries because I'm incomplete,
Though this fact I try to hide.

I miss the love and peace I left,
It has been a long and crazy ride.

Through it all I can't complain
Because I've been blessed right
from the start.

What I can say is that it hurts
To be so far away from my
heart.

So I continue on my journey
Wondering if this is real or just
a dream.

That's a question that will
continue
And at night, a silent scream.

I will slowly make my way here
As long as the world we live in
is round.

There will always be a part of
me missing
Until the day I'm homeward
bound.

César E. Becerra

Highway 1 north headed home

El Que No Sufre No Progresa

Estoy pasando un momento muy difícil en mi vida;

Me consume la tristeza al igual que la alegría.

Ayer para todo y cada cosa sin fallar había respuestas;

Hoy solo hay preguntas y mi mente está en tinieblas.

No reprocho el desafío porque con certeza me hará más fuerte;

Lo que si quisiera remediar es la confusión de este presente.

Al contrario, yo agradezco cada oportunidad de caer en vida;

Mientras tenga uno ese regalo hay que apreciar cada día.

Le doy gracias al creador por darme fe y fortaleza;

Con el tiempo aprendí que el que no sufre no progresa.

Just a Chance

I have been fortunate to have accomplished things that few people expected;
My own goals are much higher than what for me, others had selected.
I have always strived for more despite the negative things that I have seen.
Graduation rates are dismal, where did hope go? Where has it been?
Did we forget about potential? What happened to the kids I knew in school?
If they were brown and lived in poverty, it is likely that they never made it through.
So many lost souls forgotten, the ones that have fallen through the cracks;
Cracks on walls you want to fix, why not fix the ones where kids fall?
I was supposed to be a statistic but I rejected what you called my destiny,
Instead I chose to prove you wrong and turn around the hate you gave me.
That hate was absorbed by my body and was transformed into pure strength,
It became my motivation; it's what showed me to be brave.
So many times that I have failed, it is impossible to recall them all.
But that hate had made me stronger; I was stronger after each fall.
It is easy to live a life when you never experience hardship;
I've had barriers all my life and somehow I learned to overcome them.
Barriers are created with your mind and with your mind you must confront them.
You can't be afraid of making mistakes you must simply seek to learn from them.
In any challenge that I have faced I have only asked one thing;
I try my hardest every day so I can enjoy what tomorrow will bring.
I don't need you to give me anything and you might never understand;
I don't need much to show you who I am . . . . all I need is just a chance.

The Measure of a Man

I am consumed with conflicting emotions yet I know that they're all real;
The joy and pride I express openly, but the sadness I conceal.
I feel great joy and pride in knowing you are becoming a man of strength and weakness;
The sadness comes from the realization that I won't be there as a witness.
Some people are born with special gifts that are revealed when it truly matters;
Your gift is the love of people, and your willingness to give to others.
Many people walk this world aimlessly, lacking passion or a purpose;
Very few live each day to the fullest, or take the time to go past the surface.
I have had the fortune many times over of meeting people that have changed me;
I can add a new name to that list now, and I thank you for what you gave me.
You remind me that I must continue to fight a battle, though that battle might never end;
We must look to where we are going but never forget where we have been.
Your courage and spirit is astounding, you get back up each time you fall;
When you feel that you have nothing, remind yourself, in your heart you have it all.
You will undoubtedly fight your own battles and in time you will surely find;
Of all the weapons at your disposal; your greatest weapon will be your mind.
Always remember that life is all about the journey, not the final destination;
Take the time to enjoy each moment and look to the world for inspiration.
You have been given the blessing of life, now it is your mission to go and live;
Trust your heart in this great journey, there is always more that you can give.
You have left a lasting impression on me, and anyone else who has come across you;
Although you soon will go away, I can assure you, we will never be without you.
My admiration for you is endless; a new challenge is now at hand:
Being willing and ready to make the ultimate sacrifice . . . . **That's the measure of a man.**

César E. Becerra

Esaí and his uncle in a Mexika Ceremonia

El Vendido

He pasado mucho tiempo buscando mi identidad;
Soy Mexicano en el Norte, tengo más de una verdad.

En mi México querido no me siento aceptado;
Por haber nacido lejos me han echado siempre a un lado.

En Estados Unidos, el que dice ser mi país,
No les interesa lo que siento y así no puedo sonreír.

Yo no controlé que color era ni el lugar donde nací;
No encontraba mi hogar y yo jamás lo comprendí.

Yo quiero mucho a mi gente con toditito el corazón;
Tú nos juzgas sin saber y sin comprender nuestro dolor.

Ya no estoy confundido, mi mente es más fuerte que una frontera;
Ya no soy quien tú recuerdas, de esa persona nada queda.

Soy orgulloso de ser Chicano, soy un líder dispuesto a crear cambios;
Yo lucho por unidad y la justicia no motivos para separarnos.

Yo seguiré luchando siempre y seguiré mi propio camino;
¿Mírate bien en el espejo . . . . y dime quien es el vendido?

Ya No Soy Esa Persona

Que rápido pasa el tiempo, ayer yo era tan solo un niño;
Tanto tiempo aprovechado pero mucho más tiempo perdido.

Tuve yo muchas derrotas en sus ojos pero no en los míos;
Yo di todo lo que tuve, pregúntele a quien me haya conocido.

Hoy estoy ya muy cansado por los años que he vivido;
Las barreras que he superado y las desgracias que he sufrido.

Todo es parte de la vida, lo bueno viene con lo malo;
Todo junto te prepara para un futuro que crees lejano.

Recuerdo ayer haber oído, "no desperdicies tus talentos";
¿Pero que si ya los usé todos, ahora con que me alimento?

Esa pregunta jamás preguntamos y hasta nos suena algo extraña;
¿Que si ya viviste todo y ya escalaste tu montaña?

¿Que nos queda por vivir, si ya recorriste tu camino?
Yo pensé que yo era el autor de mi propio destino.

Pensé que caminaba solo, y solo aprendía de mis errores;
Solo, me enfrentaba al mundo, y a mis más grandes temores.

Estaba muy equivocado porque al fin yo aprendí;
Que solo, tú no eres nada si no aprendes a vivir.

Ayer tenía yo todo, un futuro quizás sin límite;
No llegue, y no me arrepiento, pero aún me siento triste.

Hoy siento una tristeza muy extraña y no encuentro la razón;
Imagina como se siente defraudar a tu corazón.

Que rápido pasa el tiempo, pero tu herencia nunca se borra;
A quien fui ayer le pido una disculpa, ya no soy esa persona.

Un sueño que no se realiza

Es como una vela sin fuego.

En esta vida nada es fácil;

Como quisiera ser vaso nuevo.

Chapter 5

Gracias

Tengo sed y no es de agua;

No lo puedo explicar.

Cada día que estoy sediento

Me aleja de mi realidad.

Las Palabras de la Vida

Las palabras de la vida son para el ser como alimento;
Unas se quedan en la mente y otras se pierden con el tiempo.

Estas palabras de las cuales yo hablo no se aprenden de repente;
Pueden ser las que decidan tu destino o controlen tu presente.

Se aprenden de varias maneras, quizás en un salón de clase;
Para mí las importantes, las aprendí en otra parte.

No aprendí de libros ni cuentos, y ni clase tuve que tomar;
Yo tuve la fortuna que mi gran salón fue mi propio hogar.

La definición de "sacrificio" la aprendí cuando por años;
Mire a mi padre trabajando de sol a sol, y cuando me acariciaba con sus manos.

La palabra "injusticia" la aprendí cuando mire
La forma en que trabajaban; no tener agua teniendo sed.

"Huelga" fue una palabra que aprendí cuando era todavía un niño;
No comprendía porque gritábamos, mi alegría fue estar contigo.

"Valentía" la conocí poco a poco con acciones;
Llegaron a un lugar sin nada y enfrentaron sus temores.

La "nobleza" la aprendí cuando con el tiempo yo miraba
Que obras de caridad eran naturales y que no esperaban nada.

No se ocupa nada en regreso por que la dicha está en ayudar;
Esa lección me demostraron con su ejemplo y su manera de pensar.

La "fortaleza" la entendí cuando los mire levantarse en cada caída;
Toda su vida dieron lo máximo por vernos triunfar algún día.

Finalmente la palabra "orgullo" la aprendí cuando miré
Sus ojos de inmensa alegría la tarde en que me gradué.

Esas son solo unos ejemplos de lo mucho que he aprendido;
En el salón más grande en mi vida y la clase que siempre he tenido.

Espero yo ser buen maestro, y enseñar como lo hicieron;
Eternamente les agradezco, y demostraré cuanto los quiero.

No hay palabras ni ejemplos que yo pueda utilizar;
Para expresar lo que yo siento, aunque pudiera no diría toda la verdad.

La verdad está en mis ojos y lo que siento en mi ser;
Eso quizás jamás se expresa pero en la mirada se puede ver.

Las palabras de la vida nunca se acaban de aprender;
Mis maestros son mis padres, me enseñaron tanto sin saber.

César E. Becerra

El amor que me dio vida

Gracias

Tengo tanto que expresarles y no encuentro las palabras;
Algunas cosas nunca se dicen y se ocultan en el alma.
Cuando examino los años y pienso de todo lo que me han dado;
Se humedecen siempre los ojos, y les agradezco cada regalo.
Una palabra si viene a mi mente, la que quizás lo dice todo;
Son ustedes para mí lo máximo, son realmente mi tesoro.

La palabra de la que hablo la han escuchado en varias partes;
Pero les aseguro que nadie la siente como la siento por mis padres.
Gracias quisiera yo decirles por los abrazos y los consejos;
Lo que no entiendes de niño con los años llegas a verlo.
Gracias les doy por siempre cuidarme y protegerme del peligro;
Por quitarme siempre el hambre y a mis ojos darle el brillo.

La verdad es que tomaría tal vez el resto de mis días
Para decirles lo que siento y lo que han sido en mi vida.
Para mi han sido todo, y mi razón para luchar;
Siempre quise darles orgullo, nunca los voy a defraudar.
Gracias por su fortaleza y por mostrarme lo que es paciencia;
Me han salvado muchas veces aunque no se han dado cuenta.

Les revelo que con el tiempo los he llegado a apreciar aún más;
Hoy que los siento distantes, he aprendido a extrañar.
Eternamente les daré gracias por todo lo que me han enseñado;
En todas las metas que he logrado estaban siempre a mi lado.
Las memorias me traen lágrimas, pero son lágrimas de alegría;
Gracias por cada sacrificio, gracias por darle una oportunidad a mi vida.

César E. Becerra

El orgullo de ser su hijo no se puede expresar

El Árbol Que Mas Quiero

Un árbol para mi es bello y nos protege del calor,
Se distingue por su fortaleza y por su eterno esplendor.

Un árbol cambia con los años pero su nobleza sigue igual,
El mundo los maltrata y el árbol sigue dando más.

Un árbol tiene muchas ramas y cada una depende de él,
Él siempre las sostiene, a todas las quiere, y es fiel.

Un árbol es un regalo, de nuestra tierra y del Señor,
Nos da vida, nos limpia el aire, y nos refugia con amor.

Nunca le podremos agradecer como realmente se merece,v
No hay palabras para expresar, y poco a poco la deuda crece.

Aun con lo dicho trataré de día con día demostrarle
Con acciones y triunfos, que gracias a él no soy cobarde.

Tengo el valor para enfrentarme al mundo y lo que algún día pueda llegar,
Me ha enseñado mi destino y que un hombre puede llorar.

Es imposible no ser fuerte teniendo las ganas se superar;
Esa lección también le debo, y la de "siempre hay que luchar."

Hoy le doy gracias a ese árbol, al que más quiero yo en mi vida,
Quizás nunca podré enseñarle, que me levanto en cada caída.

Hoy le confieso yo a mi madre que ese árbol ella es,
Estará siempre presente en mí, aunque sus ojos no me ven.

Mi Madrecita Querida

La Sombra de mi Viejo

La vida es un camino que el destino nos regala;
Sin saber, la vida viene; y sin saber también se acaba.

Ese camino con el tiempo te trae alegría y dolor;
Pero aun así lo tienes todo cuando la vida te brinda amor.

Amor sincero lo he sentido desde el día que yo nací;
Por mucho tiempo lo ignoraba pero en un momento lo entendí.

En la vida para un hombre, lo más difícil es llorar;
El mundo nos enseña que las lágrimas debe uno ocultar.

En mi vida yo he aprendido una lección mucho más grande;
El salón y ese maestro fue mi hogar y fue mi padre.

Mi viejo con su ejemplo me enseño que el pasado hay que dejar;
También que en esta vida, nunca es muy tarde para cambiar.

Con el tiempo me dio la valentía para enfrentar a mis temores;
Y la certeza de que cada día puedo aprender de mis errores.

Su sabiduría sin duda, en un momento me alejo de algún peligro;
Espero que en el futuro no tan lejano, yo también sea un padre digno.

Sus lecciones son una sombra que siempre me guarda compañía;
Él ha cumplido con sus deberes, la oportunidad ahora es mía.

La sombra de mi viejo la llevaré siempre a mi lado;
Ni en una vida le agradezco todo el cariño que me ha dado.

César E. Becerra

La humilde mirada de mi jefe

La Cuenta Que Jamás se Pagará

Le brindaste la esperanza a él cuando llego aquí con nada;
Lo aceptaste, y lo ayudaste a salir de donde estaba.
Poco a poco te dio sus años y tú lo ayudaste a salir adelante;
Pero él puso más de su parte, él fue el que supo ayudarse.

Tú y él juntos lograron realizar un grande sueño.
Él pudo tener su familia y tú seguiste siendo su dueño.
Él te agradece por la oportunidad de tener éxito que tú le has dado;
No comprende que fue su lucha, y su sacrificio en el pasado.

Hoy la historia ha terminado y yo te escribo de su parte;
Él no puede hacerlo ahora y para regresar ya es muy tarde.
Te agradezco lo que nos diste, quizás sin ti sería distinto,
Pero nunca te perdonaré por lo que me hiciste desde chico.

Todo lo que tú crees que nos has dado no lo podemos repagar;
Pero lo que tú nos debes es más grande y hoy te lo voy a revelar.
Él te pagó con su sudor, su sangre y con años de dolor,
Todos los días lluviosos, los días fríos y aún más los de calor.

Él dio su vida a cambio de que para mí hubiera futuro;
Él es el verdadero héroe en esta historia, eso firmemente te aseguro.
Me quedarán siempre recuerdos de cuando era niño y lo esperaba en la
ventana,
Y los días que me persignaba ya dormido en mi cama.

Los días que mostró paciencia y aun cansado me escucho,
Y las veces que sin palabras me demostró su gran amor.
Él está siempre presente, y no le debe a nadie nada;
A él realmente le agradezco y lo llevo siempre en mi mirada.

Hoy comprendo que no debemos nada porque la cuenta se pagó;
La tuya todavía está pendiente y él siempre la ignoro.
Él te agradeció por años por darme ropa y quitarme el hambre;
En cambio tú ni en una eternidad me pagas por quitarme a mi padre.

Amigo del Campesino

La labor más importante es la que a veces menos se aprecia;
Yo lo he visto con mis propios ojos, y la verdad me trae tristeza.

La tristeza viene cuando pienso que todavía hay mucho que cambiar;
Tantos logros por La Causa pero nos faltan muchos más.

Dios nos dio un angelito para que viniera a cuidarnos;
Con su pasión y su nobleza mucho pudo regalarnos.

Regalos que aun siendo merecidos siempre nos habían negado;
Un contrato justo, agua, y ser tratados como humanos.

Tan pronto como vino, nuestro señor no lo quito;
Fue un día triste de primavera cuando mi héroe murió.

Que ironía que fue en primavera, la temporada de hacer cambio y renacer;
Tanta esperanza que había sembrado, y la cosecha será nuestro deber.

El cuerpo es el que muere porque el espíritu seguirá;
La lucha sigue siempre, aunque nuestro líder ya no está.

Aun lo siento yo presente porque vive en ti y en mí;
Cuanto daría para que él viviera, yo nunca lo conocí.

Muchas gracias César Chávez, muchas gracias gran amigo;
Siempre serás mi inspiración y el ángel que siempre habías sido.

Tienes todo mi respeto, admiración y mi infinito cariño;
Sinceramente te agradece el hijo de un campesino.

Has cambiado mi presente;

El pasado está olvidado.

He conocido a mi otro yo

Gracias por estar siempre a mi lado.

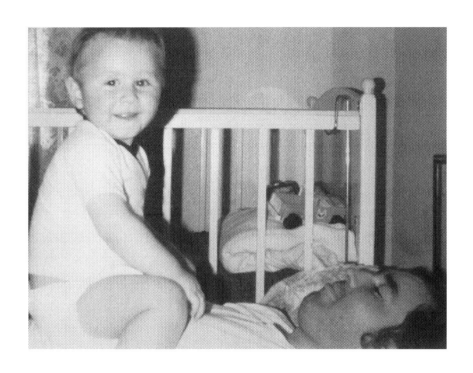

El brillo en mis ojos viene de todo su cariño

Chapter 6

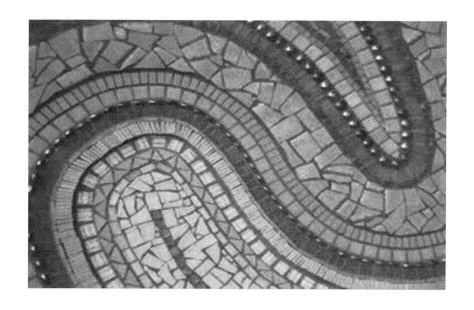

I Never Told You

Llega el atardecer; y él piensa: Se pregunta el ¿por qué no puede verla?
Los dos habitan el mismo cielo;
Los dos alumbran en obscuridad;
En general, los dos inalcanzable, como pocas cosas;
Los dos regalan mucho, y reciben poco.
A los dos no apreciarán
Hasta que dejen de brillar;
Cuánto daría él por conocerle, y compartir su soledad.

Teniendo tanto en común es injusto
El no conocerle.
Pero quizás sí se conocen, aunque los ojos
No se vean,
Quizás estuvieron juntos alguna vez,
Aunque la gente no lo crea.

Hoy se conocen sólo en sueños,
Cuando su soledad los deja.
Su soledad, en silencio, y se mantiene escondida;
Aunque quisieran ellos gritarla, a nadie le importaría.

Y si el sol duerme por las noches
Y la luna en el día . . .

Quizás es destino que así sea;
Su destino no incluye la alegría.

Y así, llega la madruga; y ella piensa . . . .

Sol y Luna

Soy un hombre muy afortunado

WHAT YOU MEAN

Few people stop to admire beauty or
Appreciate what is around them;
We take so many things for granted,
We search for our souls in order to find them.

We have so much love to share
But all too often we never show it.
The light of life surrounds us yet
We live in blindness and never know it.

I fell victim to routine and
Ignored what was important;
I need to learn to be less critical
And go back to being supportive.

Our love is like a flower;
If we nurture it, it will grow.
I have never loved like I love you;
This is one of the few certainties I know.

I've taken the time to be introspective
And came to a startling realization,
I have forgotten what you mean to me;
And my new mission is to remember.

My life has two major chapters;
There are two periods in my life:
Who I was before I met you;

César E. Becerra

And the time after you gave me real sight.

My perspective on what is beauty changed

That September day when I met you.

From that day forward you were the standard;

The one that brought my heart salvation.

Thank you for being the person that I was searching for.

Thank you for helping us form a home.

Thank you for bringing our children into the world.

Thank you for never leaving me alone.

If you are wondering what you mean to me

Because I haven't said it in so long,

I can assure you that you mean the world to me;

You are the reason why we are strong.

You have redefined the word "beauty" and

Our family has given my life meaning.

You and my boys are everything to me;

The one thing always worth believing.

I love you now more than ever

And despite our flaws I always will.

Our journey together continues,

I can't wait to see what it might bring.

I wonder when my vision left me;

I wonder when my life will end.

I wonder when the world stopped caring;

I wonder where all my dreams went.

From the moment that I met you,
I knew my future was in your eyes

Por Si Acaso Existe Duda

El amor es algo bello; algo que se tiene que apreciar;
Lo considero como un regalo que para algunos nunca vendrá.

Tienes que correr con suerte y seguir siempre tu camino;
Aunque te desvíes y te tropieces sigue siempre hacia tu destino.

Mi destino fue quererte, un día de otoño lo entendí;
Se me olvido por un instante y me acorde cuando me fui.

Desde entonces me propuse a siempre estar yo a tu lado;
Eres todo lo que necesito, eres mi futuro, y me aliviaste del pasado.

Hoy no temo a mi destino, porque al fin ya te encontré;
Te busqué toda mi vida, hoy me enseñaste a tener fe.

Tantas cosas que me has dado, no hay palabras para explicar;
Eres quien me hizo completo, eres mi única verdad.

Pido disculpas por mis fallas, las tratare de remediar;
Nunca quisiera hacerte daño, sería como yo solo hacerme mal.

Eternamente te agradezco por lo que has sido y lo que serás;
La persona que me cambio y la que le traerá a mi alma paz.

Nos encontramos justo a tiempo y gracias a eso no me perdí;
Por si caso existe duda hoy confieso que hablo de ti.

La imagen que formaliza nuestra unión

I Never Told You

I never told you that you saved me from the moment that I met you.

Everything before you was blurry; you helped me form some motivation.

I never told you that you changed me. Before, I couldn't understand feelings;

Now I am open and am not afraid to show them, you helped begin my inner healing.

I never told you that I needed you although I have shown you in many ways;

At that point it was hard for me to say it, but I felt it many days.

I never told you that I am sorry, the way that I truly felt it.

Some words and actions caused you pain and I can assure you, I never meant it.

I never told you that I love you until it was almost just too late.

Some things are so important that to express them you can't wait.

The last thing I never told you is that I love you more than myself;

I see my future in your eyes and you have given my life wealth.

I have everything I need to be happy in this world and when I realized this

my soul was new. I don't need much to be happy . . . . all I ever needed was you.

I never told you that either.

The most beautiful bride in the world

La Única Rosa Sin Espinas

Nunca he creído en lo absoluto siempre he tenido la mente abierta;
La gente sabe mucho menos de la vida de lo que piensa.

Por ejemplo les doy el dicho que no hay rosa sin espinas;
Les confieso que aun incrédulo hubo un día que lo creía.

Todo lo bello en el mundo algún día te causa pena;
No se puede amar a nadie, jugar con fuego algún día quema.

Yo iba ciego caminando por un jardín lleno de flores;
Todas eran bellas de una manera, y eran de distintos colores.

Con el tiempo fui escogiendo las que a mí más me gustaban;
Eran lindas, eran tiernas pero no me ofrecían nada.

Una noche de otoño fui caminando y la encontré;
Para mí era la más bella, y la que yo algún día soné.

Esa flor cambió mi vida y me enseñó hasta mi futuro;
Le trajo nueva luz a mi camino, y alivio mi corazón duro.

Juntos fuimos caminando y creyó que le ayude a florecer;
Pero ella siempre había sido bella, yo solo la ayude a poder ver.

Desde entonces es la única que satisface mi ilusión;
De tener lo que he deseado; compartir con alguien el amor.

Hoy no tengo más palabras que finalmente confesar;
Antes de ti yo no vivía, contigo pude empezar.

Y así cambió mi destino y comprendí que la vida es hermosa;
La única rosa sin espinas me dio su alma . . . . y hoy es mi esposa.

*"Eres la gema que Dios convirtiera
en mujer para el bien de mi vida"*

Four Seasons

First, you saved me from the memories of my past.

Then, you changed me to what I am today from what I was.

Next, you helped me every time that I felt lost.

Last, you loved me until the day that I was gone.

Whether winter, spring, or summer, and especially every fall

I was afraid to express my feelings; you helped me break down my own wall.

You were the four seasons in my life; you were everything I needed.

Some people are never forgotten; you were the one that made me see it.

César E. Becerra

Es Por Ella

Siempre quise ser una persona que reflejara una ilusión;
Quise tomar un camino único siguiendo fielmente al corazón.
Creía que de todas mis derrotas aprendía una lección;
Y cuando le falle a alguien creí que le ofrecía un sincero perdón.
Cuando llego el éxito a mi vida lo recibí humildemente;
Y cuando creí que había llegado a mi destino, logre perderme nuevamente.
Esta vida es un enigma como una pregunta sin respuesta;
La herencia que tú dejas es realmente lo que cuenta.
Descuide a quien más quiero por mis sueños de triunfar;
Sin saber que en lo más importante me resignaba a fracasar.
No tenía el balance en mi vida que es esencial para ser feliz;
Mi mente nunca descansaba y no me dejaba ni dormir.
Con la vida fui aprendiendo mientras cambiaba de niño a hombre;
Quiero regresar el tiempo a cuando ella sonreía al oír mi nombre.
Me propongo a ser una persona que lo daría todo por ella;
Espero nunca pierda la fe en mí, en mi alma esta su huella.
Siempre busca uno la culpa cuando la situación escala;
Lo que no entendemos muchas veces es que el tiempo sí se acaba.
Desde hoy no culpo a nadie porque solo es perder el tiempo;
Antes de culpar a alguien mirare el reflejo en el espejo.
Para el hombre hay principio y fin aunque en el mundo el tiempo corre;
En mi vida queda un deseo, que algún día me perdone.
Nunca quise hacerle daño y aun así le cause mucho;
Es por ella que me desvelo, y por su amor es por lo que lucho.

Always and Forever

Always and forever, you will have a large piece of my heart.

Your life and mine were meant to cross paths; I understood it from the start.

You are the person I imagined every time I closed my eyes.

I was fighting a losing battle; couldn't see truth through all the lies.

With you, truth was revealed and I realized I had been wrong;

I had been afraid of winning; I had been a coward all along.

You taught me so many lessons it's impossible to count;

You gave me inspiration; my future no longer in doubt.

I was ready for the challenges. I no longer walked alone.

Together, anything was possible; nothing can break the bond we formed.

Always and forever, I treasure you more than my life;

It's a dream to have you by my side and an honor to call you my wife.

Sometimes the image says it all

Todo lo eres Tu

Lo más difícil para un hombre es admitir sus propios errores;
Yo he sido uno de esos hombres, espero que algún día me perdones.

No sabía que te hacía daño y seguí mi vida indiferente,
Fue tan lindo nuestro pasado que me olvide del presente.

Nunca aprecias lo que tienes hasta el día que lo has perdido;
Yo no apreciaba lo que me dabas aunque tu camino siempre fue el mío.

Me dabas todo tu cariño y tu comprensión incondicional;
Yo me perdía en mi propia mente y en mi conocida soledad.

En mi corazón eras la única pero de mis labios no salía,
Creí que no era necesario porque tú ya lo sabias.

Estaba muy equivocado y como un tonto no me di cuenta;
Aunque para ti siempre estaba abierta con el tiempo serré la puerta.

Hoy quizás ya es muy tarde y reconozco que te he fallado;
Solo espero que el señor me regale tiempo para mostrar lo que he callado.

Cuando escribo no tengo miedo pero al hablar es diferente;
No me importa el riesgo que tomo ni lo que pueda decir la gente.

Desde el primer día lo supe y por mucho tiempo lo olvide;
Para cambiar nunca es muy tarde, espero que hoy me puedas ver.

Quiero ser esa persona que tú recuerdas con alegría;
La persona que te abrazaba cuando la noche estaba fría.

Hoy te confieso la verdad y casi en lágrimas me arrepiento;
El amor que a ti te tengo será eterno como la calma después del viento.

Tú lo eres todo y todo lo eres tú, este hombre ya cambió;
Gracias le daré siempre al destino por el gran regalo que a mí me dio.

César E. Becerra

Su primer día de independencia

Alegría

La alegría es una enigma, quizás jamás la entenderé;
Día y noche la buscaba y no me di cuenta cuando la encontré.

Me ha causado a mí sonrisas y llantos a la misma vez;
Nunca supe merecerla y me encontró a mí sin saber.

Duré tanto yo buscando y no entendí porque se escondía;
Mi error fue evitarla aunque creí que no lo haría.

¿Qué tipo de hombre teme algo tan bello y tan natural?
Vivía mi vida pensando que era mejor jamás amar.

El amor es lo más grande pero a la vez destruye corazones;
No quería tomar el riesgo y así vivía sin ilusiones.

Pero aun tocó mi puerta y por mucho tiempo la rechacé;
Pero al final abrí los ojos, jugué mis cartas, y al fin cambié.

Comprendí lo que era alegría, cuando a sus ojos yo miré;
Le doy gracias a mi orgullo, por ignorarlo, yo gané.

César E. Becerra

Chapter 7

¿Quién Soy Yo?

Dilemma

I am running from the future, consumed with fear of the unknown.

I am escaping from the past and the hate that you have shown.

I am afraid of my own potential; I have no places left to hide.

Lost in a whirlwind and in the fog that is my life.

I am losing my faith slowly, and feel my heart will never heal.

Sometimes I wish that I was dreaming, but my dilemma is all too real.

What will be of me?

César E. Becerra

My Greatest Mistake

In life we take on different characters hoping to one day find what we really are;

It is so easy to judge a person's actions when you are seeing them from afar.

In my life I have made so many choices that were guided by false pride;

I can't count the times I have seen wrong but lacked the courage to make it right.

I lost track of all the pain I caused not realizing who I was hurting;

I never listened to your crying heart and the relief that it was yearning.

A wise person knows their limitations and that there is so much left to learn;

I hope the flame of passion for learning inside me will always continue to burn.

Despite how much i tried to change it, I am who I am, I cannot fight it;

I love you more than life itself; today I can no longer hide it.

I apologize for the hypocrisy, for all the apologies that came too late;

Thinking that I could never change was my life's greatest mistake.

I'm sorry.

¿Quién Soy Yo?

Soy un fiel hijo.
Soy pecador.
Soy un cobarde.
Soy luchador.

¿Quién Soy Yo?

Soy una vela.
Soy el dolor.
Soy hipocresía.
Soy el amor.

¿Quién Soy Yo?

Soy estudiante.
Soy triunfador.
Soy lo más bello.
Soy lo peor.

¿Quién Soy Yo?

Soy mi futuro
Soy mi esperanza.
Soy la alegría.
Soy la añoranza.

¿Quién Soy Yo?

Yo lo soy todo.
Yo no soy nada.
No hay que temerle
A el mañana.

¿Te escucharé
Cuando me llames?
¿Quién Soy Yo?
Solo TÚ sabes.

César E. Becerra

Mi hermano Eric visitando
antiguas ruinas en México

The Person in the Mirror

Whoever told you that you are nobody couldn't see you for what you are;

The people who constantly put you down and that always did you harm.

I have tried to rid you of those demons but I have not yet made you see;

The person that I see has got the strength needed to achieve.

You see, everything that you have gone through has made you the person you are today;

You could have chosen to run and hide but you have decided to make your way.

No one ever gave you anything, except pain, grief, and self-doubt;

You have to prove all those people wrong, you have to show them that you are strong.

No one will ever truly know you the way that you know yourself;

I can tell you that I believe in you but in the wind words are often lost.

You have to believe in your future and you must fight to keep your dream;

With patience and courage you will surely get there no matter how daunting it might seem.

So keep on listening to those whispers, and those people who attempt to bring you down.

They will be your greatest motivator; they will find you wherever you are.

I have written my reality and today I finally see; the person in the mirror is finally free to just be me.

César E. Becerra

When I perish from this world;

The day that was promised from my birth;

I will leave you with a smile;

You never know how much its worth.

Who We Are

The quest for identity is everlasting;
My life has proven this as fact.

So many times I wondered who I was,
Not knowing where I had come from.

Our history is hidden in a failed attempt to blind us.
We are told to believe the world is the way that it was taught to us.

Slowly I have removed the blindfold to the point where I can see;
Gained an understanding of my ancestors, I'm alive because I bleed.

I learned to question tradition and to read between the lines;
I gained a different perspective, now I know some facts are lies.

Imperialism has left so many people starving looking for themselves;
Lonely shadows searching to alleviate the pain that you have brought.

We were native to this great land until you created a border;
Soon the oppressed will rise together, and take back what you took over.

No right can come from wrong when it's a choice not a necessity;
I hope you never experience the pain you caused, I don't believe in our
supremacy.

What I do know is that it is hard to always be the victim;
I don't seek your sympathy or charity I just want to stop being one.

We are a people now united; we will stand together as one;
You tried to keep us from the answer but now we know who we are.

Who we are: people with dreams. Who we are: People with hope.
Who we are: We are true warriors. We will soon break down the door.

César E. Becerra

My bro Fabian and my boy Pac

Lluvia

Serás una memoria siempre.
Eras el agua que creía me daba vida;
Eras quien siempre me cuidaba,
A cambio de mi propia alegría.
Llegabas siempre sin aviso.
Cuando empezaba a creer;
Cuando creía en un sol ardiente,
Pronto me venias a llover.
Cuando tenía esperanza para mañana
Aunque no encontraba calma,
Siempre estabas presente en mí,
Y confundías a mi alma.
Tanto contigo había compartido
Que ya no sentía más.
Me escondía en mis temores
Y siempre ocultaba la verdad.
La verdad es que era cobarde;
Tenía miedo de fracasar.
Sabía muy bien que había una meta
Que no tenía valor para alcanzar.
Hoy comprendo que soy el único
Que te puede hacer parar.
Te controlo con mi mente;
Algún día te he de extrañar.
Ya no quiero que estés presente,
Aunque siempre me ayudabas.
Me tenías tan engañado;
Escondía todas mis lágrimas.
Ayer busque mi alma vagabunda,
Y hoy por milagro la encontré.
Ya no oculto mis tristezas;
Hoy vivo lo que un día soñé.
Hice paz con mi propia alma;
Yo ya no te necesito.
Ahora sí puedo llorar;
Ya no tengo miedo ni frió.
Seguiré yo mi camino;
Mi destino he de ganar.
Una lección ya aprendida;
Nunca es tarde para cambiar.

Un día en la vida de un padre

Home is Where the Heart is

"Home is where the heart is"
Is a saying that in my life I never heard.
I heard it when I left you
But I never understood.
The journey taught me many lessons
Now I am older and I am wiser.
Slowly I have learned about life;
Many questions now have answers.
You never forget where you came from;
It becomes a part of your identity.
It doesn't matter where I may be,
I am still searching for serenity.
They say home is where the heart is and
that each night brings a new day.
One last question left unanswered:
Why is my heart so far away?

The town that watched me grow into a man

Nunca lo Encontraré

Siempre me acompañaba en todo;
Era mi mejor amigo.

Fue el que me salvo muchas veces,
Cuando yo estaba perdido.

Me enseñó que yo valía,
Y que lejos llegaría.

Me ayudó a comprender
Lo que ayer no entendía.

Pasaron tantos años
Y éramos inseparables.

Una unión tan especial
Que no puedo explicarles.

Sin embargo todo cambia
Y un día triste aprendí.

Tantas batallas que peleamos juntos,
Y él ya no estaba junto a mí.

Me había dejado solo,
Con un sueño y sin esperanza.

¿Qué hice para merecer su abandono?
Le hace a mi alma mucha falta.

Se fue sin decir nada
Y no lo puedo encontrar.

En las noches antes de dormir
Me pregunto dónde está.

¿Corazón porque te fuiste?
Yo intente cambiar mi vida.

No tengo ganas de seguir
Ni de enfrentar a un nuevo día.

Te extraño tanto hoy y siempre
¿Corazón donde te has ido?

Yo sin ti ya no soy nada,
¿Quién me mostrará el camino?

Estoy perdiendo la paciencia,
Poco a poco me deja la fe.

Mi temor más grande ahora,
Es que nunca lo encontraré.

Abecés las respuestas se encuentran en el
horizonte quizás fuera de nuestra vista

Myself

Who's responsible for my fortune and for knowing right and still doing wrong?
Who turned their back on my dream? Who made me weak after being strong?

Who's the person that is to blame for every time I look the other way?
Who's the one that had an opportunity but let it slip away?

Who could have made a difference but now it is just too late to know?
Who hid their feelings thinking that a man deals with his problems all alone?

Who wasted their life in the past and was too afraid to see tomorrow?
Who is to blame for all my pain? Who is responsible for my sorrow?

Who allowed me to give in when my heart wanted to fight?
Who turned the happiest of days into the gloomiest of nights?

I have lost the faith that at one point nourished me.
I don't know who or where I want to be.

With so much that is uncertain, I know that I am not happy here.
I have let my pain control me; I've sought shelter in my fear.

I don't seek your pity or sympathy, or even a second chance;
I now realize who was responsible. I must confront him like a man.

It is my shame to now reveal the answer to my questions that abound,
I now know who was responsible and I have known him all along.

Mi Destino

Tantas cosas sin respuestas;
Muchas más que no entendemos.
Unas de esas es nuestro destino;
A veces no creemos ni lo que vemos.

Siempre me he engañado solo;
Pensando que controlo yo mi vida.
Será posible que esté hambriento;
¿Estará mi alma aun vacía?

Todos tenemos un propósito
Por lo cual estamos en el mundo;
El que lo encuentra es feliz,
Y el que no, es vagabundo.

Nunca puede hacer de su alma
El hogar que necesita;
Se deja llevar por el bullicio,
Y su alma cualquiera se la quita.

Hoy entiendo que no estoy solo,
Y que a mi lado siempre hay alguien;
Alguien que siempre me cuida
Que ama sin condiciones y como nadie.

Me ha mostrado a mí un camino;
Me ha guiado sin cesar.
Ha escrito mi destino;
Pero yo lo haré llegar.

Corazón estoy perdido

¿Porque me has abandonado?

El dolor que no soporto

Es saber que te he defraudado.

*El conocimiento es el camino
hacia la oportunidad*

Chapter 8

I Will Forever Wonder . . .

In the Event of my Demise

In the event of my demise remember who I was and forget who I could have been. Every day was a blessing. Every moment was an opportunity. Every success was a struggle. Every smile gave me life and it was freedom I desired. I did the best I could with the traits that I was given. I was far from a perfect person and was never afraid to see it. My goal was to inspire minds, heal some hearts, and help hope grow. Perhaps you will someday understand that although nothing in this world is eternal my love for you was unyielding. You helped me see the world much clearer and you gave my life direction. Love became the theme of my life because that's what you created; I will forever be grateful and your impact on me never faded. In the event of my demise, please remember to always try; have the courage to stand alone and never be afraid to fly.

César E. Becerra

1978-20__

If I Don't Make it Through the Night

If I don't make it through the night please accept a sincere apology not just for all the wrong that I did but all the wrong I would have done.

I accept responsibility for all my failures as a man; I was consumed with inner darkness, waiting for an awakening that perhaps would never come.

I was searching for a destination that only existed in my mind; although my heart was always leading me; my soul always lagged behind.

I can assure that you were everything to me although I rarely conveyed it; I thank you for every memory, the love we shared never faded.

I wanted to be the person that can fill your life with joy and hope; the person that would give you wings and help let your spirit soar.

My dreams were larger than this world; yet the writing was on the wall; so many tests that life put in front of me; I can't believe I failed them all.

I wanted to bring that happiness; so elusive in your life.

I wanted to be who you needed, I simply ran out of time.

If I don't make it through the night;

Forgive me for every time I made you cry;

I was far from who you thought I was;

Please understand . . . . I always tried.

Not like father like son . . . I hope
you are a much greater man

I Have Been Ready All My Life

I have never felt truly happy;
I could never understand why.

I have been blessed my entire life
Yet I still felt a need to cry.

I was searching for a purpose;
Something to justify my existence.

Someone to prove I wasn't worthless;
Someone who would take the time to listen.

I have been searching for so long for that place where I belong;
The search has seemed eternal, like the sadness in my song.

I don't know what to expect in the days after I'm gone.
I know that I won't miss the world; I know their grieving won't be long.

I will have no choice in the matter; it will come in just an instant.
I can't fear what I don't know; I faced every challenge with
persistence.

Perhaps I'll hear that final question: Are you now ready to die?

Something needs to happen before dying;
You must at one point feel alive.

I have cried the tears I needed to cry that were caused by all the strife,
The answer to that final question: I have been ready all my life.

César E. Becerra

It rained the night I died.
I couldn't explain why?

My soul instantly rose
And became one with the stars in the sky.

A final plea of repentance,
For the wrong that I have seen.

And for not having the courage to change it,
Or at least not enough to succeed.

Success for the world was different than what it really meant to me;
I searched for more, was never satisfied, and I tried always to believe.

I believed in the future of our youth; our only hope for a better tomorrow.
I gave my life and wisdom to them; I gave them a guide that they
could follow.

I never felt my mission over;
After each challenge a new one came.

After reaching aspirations,
I set new goals and tried again.

So on my final day still breathing, I chose the right and not the wrong;
I was presented with a sacrifice and I welcomed death with open arms.

Haven't been afraid of dying since I realized that I loved God;
I have no fear of my creator; I have been witness to his love.

So I leave with only one regret;
Regret of not finishing my journey.

I will have to wait in patience
Until the day judgment comes to me.

On that day, I'll bow my head and ask why it rained that night; perhaps,
They were my own tears of joy that will someday end our plight.

Every time an angel cries, some tears fall down to the ground;
Those tears help our young seeds grow when life has got them down.

I will also ask my maker why I couldn't finish my mission;
"Coming here before me was the last stop; it was strictly your decision.

It was you who chose to fight the fight; it was you, who never wavered.
Today you reach your destination, so take pride in all your labor.

Your life was a labor of love, the most important thing in life;
You did complete your mission; today your spirit will join mine."

César E. Becerra

The fog in my life is clearing

Giving way to the sun's light

The day my life completely changed

I finally found the courage to cry.

I Never Learned to Say Goodbye

I don't know why the world is misguided
And I can't claim that I am any different.
I can assure that I always searched for truth,
Despite the pain that I have witnessed.

Maybe I will never know my purpose
Although it was a mission to achieve.
What I know is that I gave everything;
There was no more that I could give.

I always tried to create the changes
That would help our young seeds grow.
How much it hurts to not get to see it,
Is something that you might never know.

I made many mistakes along the way
But I learned from every one.
I learned to always maintain faith
And a better day will come.

I learned to stand for what you believe in;
Although it's hard it's the only way.
Listen to what is inside your own heart
Not the negative things people say.

Sometimes the truth is right in front of you
And you still would rather lie;
At times your body is full of emotion
And yet you remain afraid to cry.

So many lessons that I learned
Growing up throughout my life;
There is one that always eluded me;
The question for you today is "Why?"

Some lessons you don't learn
Until perhaps the day you die;
One more thing on the list of my regrets:
I never learned to say goodbye.

César E. Becerra

En memoria de mi abuela
1935-2010

I Will Forever Wonder . . .

There are so many questions in this world that don't seem to have an answer;
I have tried and failed daily yet I'm not afraid of what comes after.

I have been waiting to meet my maker from the day that I was born;
I did not ask to be a baby; I was brought into this storm.

Every day has been a challenge because I never looked away;
I saw what people accept as reality, I hope someday our fate will change.

Children grow up hopeless and hungry, starving for the chance to dream;
How can you teach them to be positive when wrong is all that they have seen?

Don't look too far, look around you, and count the faces with the smiles;
In my life they have been outnumbered by the sad ones for a long while.

I don't understand the world; we always want what we don't have.
We seldom take the time to be thankful for all the blessings that we have.

I can't say that I will miss it; I was searching for another place;
For a way to save my soul and overcome the challenges I faced.

I can say that at times I flew high like the mighty soaring eagle,
But other days I hit the ground with the pain of all my people.

I know now that I was too small to carry a heart as large as mine;
The burden at last was overwhelming and I acknowledged the final sign.

On my last day in this world, the day I longed for all my life;
Heavenly rain cleansed me forever; it was the most beautiful sight.

Now, I am merely an observer, I couldn't change society although I tried;
Perhaps I was born to try and fail . . . . I will forever wonder why.

César E. Becerra

Chapter 9

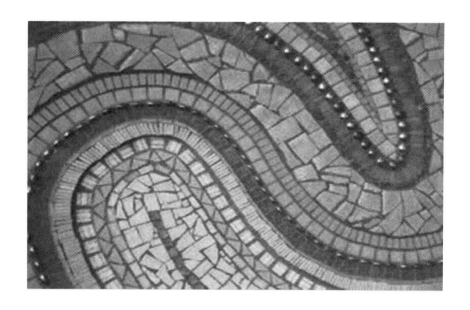

La Montaña en mi Vida

Dicen que amar y perder es mejor

Que el que nunca en su vida ha amado.

Que de la persona que pierde el futuro

¿Por no escaparse del pasado?

Con el Brillo de la Luna

En la oscuridad de mi vida ha existido una luz;
Una amiga que me cuida como la sagrada y santa cruz.

Siempre ha estado a mi lado en el momento necesario;
Siempre me ha escuchado y sin esperar nada a cambio.

Yo como humano la tome en vano y no la aprecie realmente;
Tal vez fue mi única amiga y nunca le dije frente a frente.

Hoy los días han cambiado y tengo años que no la miro;
La extraño aunque no quiera, necesito alguien conmigo.

No sé si agradecerle o condenarla a la vez;
Seguir siempre recordando o olvidarme de lo que fue.

Tantas noches le contaba los fracasos de mi vida;
No podía confiar en nadie y me brindaba valentía.

Creí yo que era fuerte pero no enfrentaba mi dilema;
Estaba muriendo yo sediento y la jarra de agua estaba llena.

Con el tiempo se hizo costumbre y me aferre a la soledad;
Tenía miedo de perderla y rechacé mi propia felicidad.

Hoy que siento la nostalgia por vivir y no haber amado;
Tengo que rehacer mi vida y alejarme del pasado.

Tengo que luchar cada día por un futuro que no es seguro;
Con el brillo de la luna, mi corazón se hizo duro.

Cuando a tu Meta Nunca Llegas

Cuando a tu meta nunca llegas hay que seguir siempre adelante;
A veces no es tan importante llegar, como el sacrificio en esforzarte.

Estas cansado y sin aliento por haber tenido tantos fracasos;
En cada caída aprendiste, te paraste y seguiste dando pasos.

Te sientes realmente vacío y piensas que nunca llegaras;
Sientes que todo lo has dado, pero si buscas valor, en ti lo encontrarás.

Solo, te has enfrentado al mundo y nunca aprendiste a confiar;
Con la experiencia as entendido que hay que buscar la unidad.

Muchos tenemos las mismas metas, juntos las podemos algún día lograr;
Tenemos que aprender a querernos y el uno al otro ayudar.

Cuando a tu meta nunca llegas, reconoce que hay que cambiar;
Tenemos que unirnos en una causa, y nuestro destino revelar.

Hasta ese momento hay que seguir, con la frente siempre en alto;
No hay vergüenza en fracasar, pero sí en no intentarlo.

Mientras tengamos un sueño, y esas ganas de triunfar;
Nadie nos quitará el orgullo, y nuestro derecho de luchar.

Hoy confieso que nunca es tarde porque el camino será muy largo;
Nuestra fuerza está en el sufrimiento de hoy y del pasado.

Con el tiempo y la esperanza estoy seguro que llegaremos;
Nada en el mundo es eterno, a la injusticia venceremos.

Your impact on my life is something you may never know

El Dolor de no Tenerte

Lo que he visto en mi vida me ha traído muchos dolores;

Tanta injusticia, ironía, el odio en tantos corazones.

Tantas veces he tratado de cambiar lo que sé que no es bueno;

Pero nunca he podido lograrlo aunque luché desde pequeño.

Muchos años han pasado pero aún no me arrepiento;

Yo di todo lo que pude, y nadie sabe lo que siento.

Aun así mi vida sigue su camino, consumida con dolor;

La razón hoy es distante . . . . extraño tanto a el amor.

Nos hacen falta tantas cosas pero en realidad tenemos mucho;

Lo que en realidad necesitamos es algo mucho más profundo.

Donde hay amor no falta nada porque el amor es poderoso;

Pero sin amor estás perdido aunque creas tenerlo todo.

Lo ignoré cuando era joven pensando que se encontraba fácilmente;

Fue el error más grande de mi vida, hoy me pierdo en el presente.

Mi pasado quiero olvidar y a mi futuro yo le temo;

Cuanto duele haber tenido y después perdido un sueño.

Our lives come and go in an instant;

I will remember where I've been.

Unfulfilled dreams will form a melody

With the whisper of the wind.

Find your Star

Why cry? Sometimes it's useless;
And it appears no one's in sight.

You feel alone with all your sorrow;
It's just you and the night sky.

Although you feel like all is hopeless;
You must search for that one star.

All it takes is one magic moment;
To heal that long time scar.

I speak solely on my experience,
For I have learned that faith is great;

César E. Becerra

When I was nothing, I gave myself to it,
And it completely changed my fate.

From that day forward all was positive
And I have refused to ever fall;

I found a dream and star to follow,
I finally took my lifelong call.

I have stopped myself from crying;
To me it was no more than wasted time.

I decided to write my destiny,
I decided to be alive.

El Valor Para Empezar Nuevo

Qué difícil es perder cuando lo has entregado todo;
Sientes que es el fin del mundo y te sientes tú muy solo.

Que injusticia haber luchado y no lograr la recompensa;
Las historias deben terminar alegres, que grande es esta tristeza.

¿Qué lección puedo aprender de mi más grande derrota?
Hice todo lo que pude hacer y parece que a nadie le importa.

¿Tu propia opinión es la que cuenta, te crees perdedor o ganador?
Lo que piense de ti la gente no tiene el mismo valor.

Que se ganan con juzgarte, tú eres el único que entiendes de tu esfuerzo;
Tú te enfrentas a los obstáculos, cuando ellos te creen desecho.

Mucho puedes tú ganar hasta en la más dura caída;
Sabiduría que algún día hasta podría cambiar tu vida.

Un día yo sin esperarlo comprendí que era muy cierto;
Cada caída que yo daba me hacía fuerte como el alimento.

Una cualidad muy grande, que hoy conmigo siempre llevo;
Es lo que encontré al levantarme; el valor para empezar nuevo.

La mejor manera de aprender a caminar

La Montaña en mi Vida

Todo me parece un sueño, voy subiendo una montaña;
Estoy subiendo muy despacio el viento dificulta más la hazaña.

Varias veces me he caído pero es la ley de la experiencia;
De esa manera se aprenden lecciones, y se cultiva la paciencia.

El camino se me ha hecho eterno, y tengo años intentando;
Parece que no me he movido pero al mirar atrás, voy progresando.

Con el tiempo tuve victorias y aun tuve más fracasos,
Pero en la vida de todo se aprende mientras sigas tomando pasos.

De repente llega la hora y al fin he llegado a la cima:
Finalmente lo he logrado, y así termina mi vida.

Es la única montaña que cuando subes nunca bajas;
Ya no puedes subir más, y ya jugaste tus barajas.

Lo más bonito de esta aventura es que la puedes compartir;
Puedes dejarles una herencia a la juventud que está por venir.

Ese fue mi gran orgullo, saber que riqueza sí deje;
No la riqueza que tú conoces, la que no se puede ver.

Conquisté yo esa montaña, y seguí caminando aunque me cansé;
Un sacrificio muy pequeño, que hoy les quita esa sed.

Todos nosotros estamos sedientos, y buscamos sabiduría;
Poco a poco se consigue, y con sus triunfos, mi alegría.

Esta es la historia autentica de la montaña en mi vida;
Y así terminó mi camino eterno, hacía la sabiduría.

*Siempre estaré dispuesto y listo
para escalar nuevas montañas*

Eternal Friend

I don't know why you left me,
You were there when I began.

You were there when I was lonely,
Always reminding me that "I can!"

I can do so much that I never thought;
Things that people would not believe.

You showed me passion you gave me spirit;
It will always live in me.

You taught me many lessons you did not intend to teach;
Love and friendship teaches lessons that only your heart can truly see.

So thank you for all you have given me;
You gave me the wings I need to fly.

I'll never know why they took you from me;
I will forever wonder why?

So I express to you my gratitude, I can never say goodbye;
I have a dream now to achieve, and you will always be by my side.

You came to me in the beginning and you will be with me until the end;
Deep bonds and roots are never broken, goodnight eternal friend.

"Although things change, the future is still inside of me.
You must remember that tomorrow comes after the dark,
And you will always be in my heart with unconditional love." T. Shakur

Your support and understanding means more than you can imagine

Como Duele

Como duele tener una meta sin el valor para alcanzarla;

Tener la alegría en frente de ti y no poder apreciarla.

Como duele ser vencido nuevamente por no creer.

Como duele estar rodeado de belleza y no tener ojos para ver.

Como duele tener esperanza si no te animas a soñar;

Tanto dolor que a mí ha venido y es imposible regresar.

El futuro aún es posible, pero el pasado debes dejar;

El pasado ya está escrito y ya nadie lo puede cambiar.

Tu futuro es una hoja en blanco que con el tiempo llenarás;

Aunque no lo creas ahora, los años y la experiencia te cambiarán.

Como duele vivir en el mundo no apreciando cada día.

Como duele ser un joven perdido, y tener el alma vacía.

Tantas penas e injusticias que nunca podré entender;

Como duele ser alegre, tenerlo todo, y no saber.

César E. Becerra

So many roads for me to choose from

Which one will guide me home?

I can't ask you to help me choose it

I must find it on my own.

No Me Canso . . .

No me canso de mirar esas sonrisas vagabundas;
Ni el brillo de los ojos cuando una mirada es profunda.

No me canso de creer que todo pasa por un motivo;
Y cuando todo parece oscuro alguien alumbra otro camino.

No me canso de sentir que todo mi esfuerzo fue en vano;
¿Qué orgullo existe en ser fiel y sentirte abandonado?

No me canso de desear que tomen un camino bueno;
Aprecien lo realmente importante, lo material es lo de menos.

No me canso de llorar aunque no hay lágrimas en mis ojos;
Por afuera yo lo escondo pero por dentro estoy muy solo.

No me canso de creer que en todo lugar hay esperanza;
Cuando hay amor y fe en su alma, en la vida nada falta.

No me canso de sentir que hay nobleza en todos lados;
Espero no despertar del sueño y estar equivocado.

No me canso de extrañar las nuevas memorias de cada día;
La que quisiera olvidar es la de la triste despedida.

Espero que algún día y nunca sientan lo que siento en este momento;
La alegría de renacer y la tristeza de perder un sueño en el viento.

No me canso . . . . Y no me cansare. Seguiré tomando pasos.

El orgullo de ser padre es algo que
no tiene medida

Pain

There is a pain that comes from trying when it's never quite enough;
Frustration overcomes you and even easy steps seem tough.
There is a pain that comes from falling especially after climbing very tall;
The more success that you experience, the more you feel the day you fall.
There is a pain that comes from living and just from opening your eyes;
So much wrong you witness daily, you are tired of hearing all the cries.
All these pains I experience daily, sometimes I find no place to hide;
Sometimes I feel there is no tomorrow and question the meaning of my life.

All this hurt has taken a toll on me and it almost brought me down;
But I refuse to let it beat me, I searched for courage and I have it now.
In this world pain is eternal, always present just like hope;
Opportunity is always knocking; you have to learn to open the door.
Who will win? This is the question and this pain you must outlast;
There is only one pain that I fear: The pain of giving up too fast.
I will never let you beat me. I will use you to endure.
You give me strength; you keep me going . . . I'm where I am because of you.

César E. Becerra

La ignorancia en el mundo

No es difícil de entender

Con tanta injusticia en pleno día

Ni el ciego quiere ver.

Una Guitarra Llora

Una guitarra llora porque está perdida en un bosque;
Toca su melodía pero no hay nadie que le importe.

No hay nadie que la escuche o que la quiera entender;
Se siente ella muy sola y sigue tocando sin acceder.

Sigue adelante porque aun estando vacía;
Se llena con la esperanza de que alguien escuche algún día.

Su ritmo ha cambiado con el tiempo por lo que ha visto con sus ojos;
Su alegría y tristeza es infinita; como ella sienten pocos.

Aún así no se arrepiente y regalará su música por siempre;
La melodía ira viajando hasta que llegue a nuestra gente.

Hay que llevar siempre en nosotros, la verdad que todo cambia;
Esperaré con ansiedad, el día que mi ser encuentre calma.

Tenemos que cantar juntos, y unidos cambiar la realidad;
En la unidad esta la fuerza, un día lo vamos a lograr.

Hasta que llegue ese momento continuara esta historia humilde;
Mientras exista fe en su alma, casi todo es posible.

Algún día escucharemos su melodía

Ayer Jamás Regresará

Crecimos juntos como hermanos,
Éramos inseparables.

Aunque el futuro era incierto,
Ciertos momentos son inolvidables.

Aunque vivíamos lejos,
La distancia no era nada.

Caminado o en bicicleta,
Las millas eran como pulgadas.

Pronto fuimos creciendo,
Ya no éramos lo que ayer habíamos sido.

Ya no éramos inocentes,
El mundo habíamos conocido.

En mi vida he aprendido mucho,
Pero mi más grande lección:

Todo cambia con el tiempo,
Llegará el día de decir adiós.

Hoy vivimos como extraños,
Aunque siguen en mi mente.

Guardo memorias del pasado,
Cuando la unión aún era fuerte.

No creí que llegara el día
Cuando perdiera a mis amigos.

Ya somos otras personas,
Tomamos distintos caminos.

Sin embargo extraño tanto,
Quizás nunca lo entenderán.

La vida se vive para el futuro,
Ayer jamás regresará.

Chapter 10

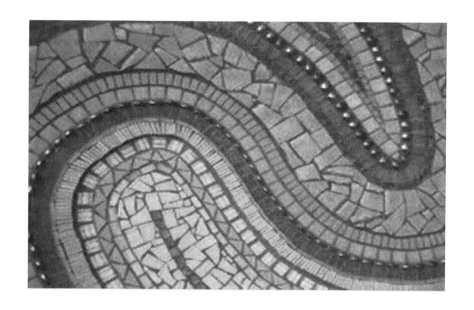

Almost

Dear Mama,

The world just doesn't get it;
I was born and lived a dreamer
But the nightmare is what I'm seeing.
Condemned for my beliefs that our people could fly high;
Just because we are different doesn't mean that we should hide.
I'm not hiding from this world, and could care less what they might think;
Listening to my own voice is the only way to succeed.
Success is so subjective; true success is in your heart.
People merely judge you and try to keep you in the dark.
They choose to live in ignorance, indifferent to society's ills,
"What I don't know won't ever hurt me" is how a lot of people feel.
From today forth I'm making changes; rules of society no longer apply.
I will live by rules of empathy; I will no longer feel them cry.
I've felt the tears of all my people; I have felt them for many years.
I fear the day that I give up; I know this day is not yet near.
Hope and spirit quenches thirst and it certainly feeds your soul;
These two things I will from now on live with until the day my heart turns cold.
Better days will someday greet me, I sure hope I live that long.
I'll live my life the way I want to; fighting against what I feel wrong.
I want to leave a better world than what it was when I first came;
Will I live to see some changes or will my struggle be in vain?

Sincerely,

Your lost son who now is found

César E. Becerra

My boy and his uncle deep in thought

One Race

I still believe in happy endings, I still think dreams can be achieved. I feel that we will overcome until the day that we are free. I feel we are marginalized people, I can feel we are not the same. Even if I didn't feel it, it's in your media night and day. Few Latinos in the movies, many of them are on the news. You can't fool me any longer; I put together all the clues. Have you not learned from our history? By "our", I mean the human race. The world is much bigger than this country, open your eyes, you'd be amazed. Our problems pale in comparison with the ones across the world. We complain about such trivial things; most people would trade places if they could. Look at our track record of oppression, of violence, and senseless hate; our country is the best in the world but there is so much that we must change. Why does the rest of the world hate us? Have you ever stopped and wondered? We kill off entire villages and then we claim to alleviate hunger. Have you heard of Agent Orange? What about Hiroshima, or Vietnam? There is so much pain that we have caused and there is no turning back the clock. We can't change what is already written but we can learn from our mistakes; we were all meant to share this world. We are one; the human race.

César E. Becerra

Almost

I have almost reached my destination, and reached the goals that I
have set;
Those goals have never been to help myself, they were meant to
create change.

I have almost been defeated times in the past but I've survived;
It is those times that we have our backs to the wall that lead to the
biggest fight.

I can see we are almost equal because we have progressed through
the years;
I am thankful for those who came before me; I am thankful for
their tears.

It's those tears and years of struggle that have allowed our
generation to grow;
I truly feel that they are heroes; they have opened so many doors.

Social change slowly approaches; our people have risen from their
sleep;
It took years of oppression to realize that unity is what we need.

Now there is still one final issue, the issue of freedom is at hand;
It was written two hundred years ago in the "supreme law of the
land."

I can see some subtle changes, but the truth is almost clear;
Although we are said created equal in some minds we still cause fear.

Are we free to pursue happiness? Are we free to live a healthy life?
Do we have liberty in this nation? Or are the creeds just shameless
of lies?

You can count all of our successes and believe that we are almost free;
But you have not been given anything; you have worked for it
can't you see?

You have worked for a better future. **You** have worked to
persevere.
Despite it all we are still not equal, sadly . . . even almost, is not
yet here.

Street mural in the Mission District

Cages or Wages

You say that there is equality
And that people here are free.
I wonder who you speak about;
You are not speaking about me.
My people have always struggled
To get the little that they have.
They have given more than taken
Yet the truth is very sad.

The truth is that very little has changed
Since the fight for civil rights.
Today, racism is subtle,
But we can read the hidden signs.
We are not free to pursue happiness
In a place where ignorance reigns supreme.
Our children don't have equal opportunities;
Only a small portion succeed.

You have left us just two choices;
Just two ways of being trapped.
One day the tables will be turned;
One day you'll feel what we feel inside.
So please take the time to see us
As people not just as races,
But until then our two choices remain:
Locked in cages or trapped in wages.

César E. Becerra

Empty Promises

I live in a free country.

I am free to pursue happiness.

I live a life of liberty.

I can't see any poverty.

My home is good and almighty.

We never make mistakes.

Mistakes are for mere mortals.

We are not the same.

This land was not stolen

It was bought at a bargain.

Believe what you read in history

The truth is far too alarming.

A new age is upon us perhaps

This era will bring change.

Maybe things will be different

Or maybe just more of the same.

So the pressure keeps building

And our stress will keep mounting.

Stop feeding us empty promises,

Change is what we are demanding.

There is no shame in trying and failing

Or even coming very close

Trying is the only way to have a chance

When you fail to try, you'll never know.

True change never comes easy

Nobody Cares

There is so much wrong in the world. The world is full of people starving. We have children killing children, reading the newspaper is alarming.

I don't like to watch TV anymore because the dial is full of trash you can't imagine. This is what our kids are watching; learning your values through it is almost tragic. What do kids have to look forward to? Every generation is subject to more danger and negativity. I'm tired of hearing things can't change and that it is not our responsibility. We are not responsible for creating changes but we **are** responsible for trying. Have you embraced inevitable hate or are you tired of victims crying? We always have the choice to do or not do something. We choose whether or not to care. We are robbing them of a future and I am convinced that it is not fair. Our children are our most valuable resource and take a look at what we teach them. Most of us don't even have the time to attempt to even reach them. We teach them to be greedy, be apathetic and to value material possessions. How about teaching the lessons of always working hard and valuing education? "Nobody cares" is what they tell me and looking closely, it has been true most of my life. When presented with the chance to be courageous most people would rather run and hide. I am hopeful that one day soon we'll find the people who **do** care. I will finish with more questions: Please tell me when and where? "Nobody cares", this needs to change I think to myself while glancing at the moon.

Nobody cares has been the problem . . . . How about starting change with you?

Why aren't we following their example?

Spare Change?

I'm in a dream I've had before yet something is not the same.
I'm trying to find my way back home but can't remember where I came.
I feel lost and alone, I walk in silence and I am amazed at what I see.
Normal things we ignore daily, is this really just a dream?
So many broken promises, so many dreams forgotten;
So much senseless hate in the world; it is time for us to stop it.

I keep walking past a field where a lot people labor.
Sun to sun is the standard work day and this person can be your neighbor.
These people work twice as hard as the ones in suits and ties,
But when it comes to yearly wages, salaries just allow them to survive.
They essentially give up their lives so we can have food on our table.
Why don't we take the time to thank them? Why don't we appreciate their labor?

Then I walk past a school and I see that there are children playing.
I stop and wonder about the future, I wonder if anyone is praying.
Is anyone praying for their future and is there hope for their tomorrow?
Their faces are full of life and joy today. Tomorrow will they be full of sorrow?
Kids grow up without examples and they rarely learn to dream.
A sad reality that haunts me, I wish I could make them all believe.
We have to raise the expectations; children will undoubtedly try to reach them.
We have to educate them together; it is our responsibility to teach them.

Parents are the most important teachers. Many children teach themselves instead.
We have to look out for all children; we need to make compassion spread.
Don't sign up if you aren't ready, your child is not to blame for your mistake.
Look at the job description before applying; do it for the child's sake.
Nothing sadder than a child asking for their parents and why they have to live

so poor. Whatever you may think it takes to be a parent, I can assure you that
it's much more.

I continue on my journey; I see a dedicated teacher struggling to pay the bills.
With such a large responsibility, can you imagine how it feels?
Trying to teach and make a living? You can't make it on one wage.
A teacher has to get a second job to make it? We should truly be ashamed.
The teaching profession is one of caring and it's a profession based on love.
We should hire and keep the best. We should all thank them from the heart.

Now the sun is slowly vanishing, soon the night will be fully dark.
I turn the corner into the "bad neighborhood", alarmed with what I saw.
I found 3 police cars together; I saw their flashing lights;
I saw the streets taped off in yellow; I saw a body outlined in chalk.
I saw many people crying; I saw a kid die for no reason;
I saw a mother torn to pieces; another casualty of the season.

Despite it all the haze won't leave me, and I continue moving forward.
This path looks so familiar but to this point has led me nowhere.
I am more lost than ever, I have no idea where I am going;
I apparently step foot on gang "turf", gang signs are proudly showing.
The writing is on the wall, the anger is visible in their eyes;
The hate is slowly killing them; the victims are you and I.
Why can't we just come together and realize there is just one color?
I hope I live enough to see a change when we can see each other as brothers.

I move on a little faster; now I am conscious of my safety;
I continue walking aimlessly to see another form of slavery.
I see girls like ones that you know, perhaps lacking self-esteem;
As a society we create them and then their fate we can't believe.
Their parents were never present or very likely involved with drugs;
Some were victims of abuse; cold shoulders quickly replaced the hugs.

In time they reach their breaking point and desperately search for a way out;
There is immense sadness in their eyes and in their voice a silent shout.
Many of them resort to selling pleasure, along with dignity and their pride;
I can't judge them without knowing them. I could only wonder why.

On the opposite side of the same street I see people selling dope;
Then I see the result of their business: I see the junkies lacking hope.
They have chosen to do wrong, but for some it's the only option;
Some must make a living at any cost and live day by day in caution.
Why would anyone sell drugs? Perhaps to survive or fight starvation;
Unless you've had your back against the wall, you probably shouldn't pose the question.

Finally, I see a beggar, with infinite wisdom in his eyes.
A complete stranger that looks familiar; much to my surprise.
You can see the pain he carries through a jar he carries with change.
Yet you can see the hope he holds; the combination appears strange.
With a look I've never seen before he holds the jar up to my chest.
I hear a melodic whisper. Without a word he asks me for spare change.

At that moment I lost all consciousness and it appeared like I was dying.
Perhaps I was awaking or maybe my soul was crying.
My eyes closed for no reason; my body lost all its feeling.
Conflicting emotion overtook me; my wounded heart had started healing.
With the little strength left in my body, I attempted to open my eyes.
After a few seconds of trying, I suddenly see a flash of light.
Then the light became much brighter, like I was staring at the sun.
I had a simple choice to make then. Should I stay or should I run?

I decided to stay and face the light that gave true vision to my eyes.
I caught a glimpse of the Creator; I swear that he was in plain sight.
"You have time for just one question" he whispered slowly like before.
A once in a lifetime opportunity was knocking; I just needed to find the door.
I remembered what he asked me, and I envisioned how he felt;
I tried to put myself in his position, and in one motion down I knelt.

César E. Becerra

At this point our eyes were level and for the moment we were equal; Any judgment I had before left me, we were just two common people. He had asked me for some change; the kind we often take for granted. The same change that eludes us or perhaps the one I have always wanted. At that moment there was no doubt whatsoever, and the question finally came.

Staring straight into those majestic eyes . . . . I asked our savior for the same.

Sadly, some dreams are all too real. ***Spare Change?***

Illegal

How can a person be illegal just for trying to feed their kids?
Are you illegal for exploitation and for trying to feed your greed?

How are these people harming you, in comparison to what you have done?
You have shattered hope in their home countries; are you not the guilty one?

It's ok to downsize factories, and to violate a worker's rights;
But when you try to point the finger, you expect us not to fight.

You leave my people no choice, except to come to a new place;
All the people you call immigrants, are the ones that put food on your plate.

We don't fight you with our money, because we don't have much of that;
What we do have are dreams and a heart, did you forget what that was like?

Are you not another immigrant who came to this country seeking change?
Just because your skin is lighter aren't our actions just the same.

You embrace us when you need us, like in the Second World War;
When you were desperately needed cheap labor, you "graciously" opened your door.

How many of our soldiers have fought for you, and for your red, white, and blue?
Giving up your life is the ultimate sacrifice; did you forget all those lives too?

Is this not enough for you, please think about this, and of our fate;
We not only gave our lives for you we helped to make this nation great.

I don't hate you or despise you, but I sure hope you someday see;
The people you call ILLEGAL have hopes and dreams; no different from
you and me.

César E. Becerra

*My feeling heart places humanity
before patriotism*

You and 1

Take a good look at your situation and then compare it to the one we are in;
Do you think that you a citizen? Do you think you are free of sin?

Our stories are more similar than what you would like to think;
History books are not all accurate, they are just words written in ink.

Those words come from a perspective; from human minds and thus they are flawed.
You can't believe everything you read; you must see it with your own eyes.

I have read that there is equality. I have read that we are free.
I have read that we have equal rights, but with my eyes I've never seen.

We have been marginalized people; all my life this has been true.
What surprises me is that you don't see it; you are part of this group too.

Look at all the people around you; what do you see behind their smile?
They never take the time to know you though they have seen you for a while.

Am I ashamed of being born different? Am I ashamed of what I am?
Prouder than this I couldn't be; you're the one that needs to change.

Look deeper than what you see on the surface; try to focus on what's inside.
You will see the things you learned before are all falsehoods . . . they are just lies.

What amazes me is your ignorance, and that you point your finger and blame;
Despite our differences please realize . . . you and I . . . We share our pain.

César E. Becerra

The Colors on my Canvas

The vibrant colors of the world make me
Grateful for the sense of sight;
Without the full colors in the spectrum
We could not appreciate light.
Red and Blue have been significant
On the canvas of my life;
Colors that have caused me great pain
And are at the center of my strife.
Red and Blue are beautiful colors
That have gradually been distorted;
Red and blue are in our history
And in the tragedy that has unfolded.
One is the color in our blood
And represents our strength and pride.
How and when did we forget this?
Why couldn't we read the warning signs?
The other is the color of our sky and ocean;
Representing trust and wisdom.
We turned a positive into a negative
And fell victim to the system.
Red represents the fire inside me,
And the passion in my heart.

Blue is the color of my sadness
Because we choose to embrace the dark.
They say red and blue can't coexist
Because they contrast or are just too
Different;
"Can't" should not be in our vocabulary.
Using the mind as the weapon,
We must always be persistent.
Red and Blue CAN come together,
And our history could come full circle;
We were once a people of majestic grace,

When united, these two colors can yield purple.
Purple is the color of royalty;
It's the color of you and me.
To me it has a special meaning:
It's the color of my dream.

*The Eagle Warrior inside us has
the capacity to conquer all*

Chapter 11

The Time Is Now

Con El Tiempo Todo Cambia

Con el tiempo todo cambia:
He escuchado toda mi vida.

¿Cuándo cambiara mi tristeza?
¿Cuándo se convertirá en alegría?

Mira bien como vivimos,
Y dime que es lo que ha cambiado.

¿Qué futuro nos espera?
¿Por qué no aprendemos del pasado?

Me alimento de esperanza
Porque de injusticia ya me llené.

Tantas luchas terminaron en fracasos
Pero aun así luché.

Con el tiempo todo cambia;
Es certeza, pero me pregunto:

Tantos años esperando,
¿Cuánto tiempo es lo justo?

Estoy cansado de esperar, a esa hora que no ha llegado;
Hoy comprendo que es AHORA; el cambio está en nuestras manos.

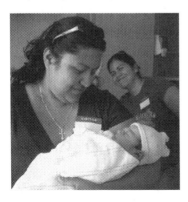

The Gift

There is a gift that keeps on giving that I took for granted in the past;

There came a point in my life when I realized that this gift perhaps won't last.

You never know what you have until the day that it is gone;

Every day is a new blessing and every trial makes us strong.

The gift I speak of is priceless and it isn't wrapped nicely in a box;

If you appreciate this gift fully it will open many locks.

The doors of possibility are locked by our own imagination;

The gift allows us to see this and to seek out inspiration.

You are often the person that places limits on your potential;

Never fully understanding that believing you can do it is monumental.

Once you believe in your abilities, your destiny will slowly unfold;

Always take a moment to be thankful and never sell your promise short.

The gift I speak of is all around us and it grows with every passing day;

We have a choice to take advantage of it or to let it slip away.

Understand the power of this gift and your goals and dreams will be in range;

The gift I speak of will never leave us . . . . an opportunity to make a change.

"Seize the day and seize the gift."

Sin Temor, Con Esperanza

El camino de sus vidas no es fácil, es algo duro;
Cada paso que dan para adelante los hace sentirse más seguros.
Aprenden de sus victorias y aún más de sus derrotas;
El valor para seguir luchando es realmente lo que importa.
Día con día han escuchado lo que pueden o no pueden hacer;
Esa decisión es solo suya nadie más puede saber.
Usen todo lo negativo y denle media vuelta para así poder triunfar;
Busquen siempre las soluciones en vez de solo a quien culpar.
La verdad es que ustedes controlan el viaje a su destino;
Recuerden siempre sus valores y disfruten el camino.
Muchas piedras o tormentas los amenazará en el futuro;
Pero cada obstáculo se puede vencer aunque todo parezca oscuro.
Sin temor y con esperanza sus metas algún día lograrán;
Ustedes son autores de su destino, y si quieren, llegarán.

"Con ganas y con fe, casi todo es posible. ¡Si pueden!"

César E. Becerra

La vida es dura y tal vez injusta;

Esto lo llevo siempre en mente.

Nada en la vida es prometido,

Seguiré luchando por mi gente.

La Silla Vacía

Hoy es un día muy importante;
Se reconoce lo que has logrado.
Tanto dolor y sacrificio,
Pero al fin ya has terminado.

No sabrás cuanto me duele
No estar contigo festejando;
Fuiste un gran ejemplo para mí
Y tu logro me cambió tanto.

He confirmado mis sospechas
Que el corazón es algo grande;
Al entregarlo a algo por completo
Te das cuenta que no es justo
ignorarle.

Todo lo que creías no poder lograr
Rápidamente es posible.
Todo está en lo que piensas;
Si crees en ti, muy poco es imposible.

Pero hoy, sí estoy contigo
Aunque para los ojos estoy distante.
Estoy presente con orgullo
Y guardaré cada instante.

Quizás hoy es la despedida,
Pero para mí nada ha cambiado;
Tú seguirás peleando esa batalla
Y yo seguiré siempre a tu lado.

Quiero ser lo que te apoye
En tus victorias o derrotas;
De todo se puede aprender;
Después de cada lucha sigue otra.

Nunca dudes tu belleza;
Nunca dudes lo que hay en tu mente.
Levántate en cada caída
Y mantén en alto la frente.

Nunca podré decir adiós
Pero sí un sincero "buena suerte";
Deseo que encuentres lo que buscas;
Deseo algún día volver a verte.

Recuerda que existe alguien que te
admira
Por tu valor y fortaleza.
Espero que siempre recuerdes eso;
Nunca pierdas la paciencia.

Seguirá usted su camino;
Espero que encuentre la alegría.
Estoy con usted aunque no vea,
En cualquier silla que crea vacía.

Estaré siempre pensando
Y deseándole lo mejor;
Una sonrisa siempre es gratis
Pero tiene infinito valor.

Gracias por lo que me ha enseñado
Aunque cree que no puede ser;
Yo siempre supe que podía
Yo solamente se lo hice ver.

¡Felicidades en su día!
Su realidad está en la mente;
El futuro y su éxito,
Vendrá de las decisiones en el presente.

César E. Becerra

*The overwhelming joy of reaching
a lifelong dream*

When You are Feeling all Alone

When you are feeling all alone, try to remember that it is just a feeling;

You must accept your vulnerability before beginning the inner healing.

Time heals every wound although at times we don't believe;

Every person will overcome failure before learning to succeed.

Success is what you make it . . . it is up to every person to define;

Success is in the journey, and overcoming obstacles over time.

There is time to achieve anything if you appreciate every day;

Every moment is a gift . . . . appreciate life in every way.

When you are feeling life is hopeless, the feeling only lasts a while;

Take a breath, keep moving forward, and never be ashamed to smile.

When your journey is finally over, you will realize that you were strong;

You were never truly alone . . . . Someone was with you all along.

César E. Becerra

Aunque Creas Tener Nada

Ya ha llegado el momento, tienes que hacer una decisión:

Enfrentarte al desafío o seguir viviendo con temor.

Si lo intentas es probable que te lleve a una caída;

Pero el que no toma ese riesgo no aprovecha de su vida.

A cada uno de nosotros nos han criado con humildad y fortaleza;

En el Corazón no falta nada aunque vivimos en la pobreza.

Llega un punto en la vida cuando entiendes tantas cosas;

El pasado ya se ha ido y el presente es lo que importa.

Si pierdes la valentía de intentar, en ese punto has fracasado;

En ese momento pierdes todo, y aun tu vida no ha empezado.

Busca valentía y toma ese riesgo cuando lo tengas cara a cara;

Pierdes mucho cuando te das por vencido, aunque creas tener nada.

The Time is Now

"Don't wait until tomorrow to do what you can do today"
I heard this saying most of my life and always had something to say.
When you are young you lack experience and have a limited perspective;
Time forces us to see the world differently and makes us more reflective.
Being born with less allows you the chance to dream a little more;
Perhaps we lack material items but what's inside you can't ignore.
You have a fire within you and strength in your heart that time will show;
If you nurture your potential, you will slowly watch it grow.
Set your sights on an endeavor and take the most important step;
The first step is the hardest . . . don't be afraid to make mistakes.
Success won't be handed to you, there are many paths to explore;
Look at the image in the mirror and ask yourself: Can I do more?
Whatever road you may be walking you must be ready to accept the destination;
Take the time to make those important choices and look to the world for
inspiration.
Open your eyes and see what is out there, if you look closely you will see it;
The opportunity is right in front of you, you must find the courage to seize it.
Throw the excuses out the window and let the wind blow them away;
Hold on to hope. Keep moving forward. Don't ever let your dreams go astray.
If you are moving in the right direction, be willing to lend a hand;
When faced with the inevitable challenge, don't be afraid to take a stand.
The past is now behind us and it has taught us many lessons;
The future is uncertain so don't forget to count your blessings.
Today is a gift, perhaps it is why it's called the present;
Unwrap it slowly, appreciate it fully, and most importantly make the best of it.
No matter how bad the storm is, the sun comes out after the rain;
You want your life to be different? The time is now to make that change.

César E. Becerra

La Barca

Una barca navegaba tristemente y sin destino;
No sabía de su pasado; no sabía de su camino.

Solo sabía que se encontraba en un mar de indiferencia;
En un mar de reglas ya escritas, perdiendo la paciencia.

Una barca sin el mar no tiene ningún sentido;
Sin embargo el mar sin una barca, sigue su mismo ritmo.

Las olas, fuertes y violentas le impedían progresar;
Pero sus ganas y valentía no la dejaban fracasar.

Hubiera sido quizás más fácil navegar con la marea;
Pero sería el mar que decide el camino, la barca tenía otra idea.

Cuando sentía no poder más, buscaba fuerza en el cielo;
El sol y las estrellas le quitaban siempre el miedo.

Y así siguió adelante; ignorando sus temores, aun sin saber su rumbo;
Con sus sueños siempre en mente, y una luz que cambia el mundo.

Su meta es buscar barcas y darles luz una por una;
Juntas alumbrarán el camino, y cambiaran nuestra fortuna.

Nosotros somos la barca, nuestro mundo es el mar;
Nunca se den por vencidos; a su destino han de llegar.

"Lighting someone else's candle with yours does not
diminish your own light; together, you shine brighter."

Find the Fire

We are fighting a tough battle;
One that might not ever end.

There is so much we think we might lose,
But there is so much more to gain.

The youth are walking aimlessly,
They are looking for direction.

Why can't they see that they are special?
That's my most intriguing question.

I believe that you can do so much,
But tell me what do you believe?

The answer to this question
Will be what allows you to succeed.

You must choose your actions wisely,
You never know who might follow.

If you choose a life of integrity,
You will be the leaders of tomorrow.

You are fighting a battle also,
Although perhaps you just can't see it.

It's a fight against yourself;
And most of you cannot believe it.

It is you, who holds you down,
You create your own expectations.

You are the ones who believe the lies,
And don't seek out inspiration.

Are you looking for what's important?
Or are you just wasting your time?

There is a flame that burns inside you;
This is the FIRE that you must find.

César E. Becerra

Give Learning a Chance

When you take risks in life, you learn to live.
When you truly live, you fall down.
When you fall, you learn to get up.
When you get up, you learn to persevere.
When you persevere, you learn about success.
And when you succeed . . . you'll see that you had it in you all along.

Give learning a chance and you will find what you are looking for;
Give learning a chance and you will never again be who you were before.

Tu Puedes

No mereces lo que sufres,
Quizás todo sea una prueba;

Y al final de esa jornada,
Consigas lo que más deseas.

La esperanza es tu amiga,
Y en la que tienes que confiar;

Pasos firmes hacia adelante,
Y nunca mires hacia atrás.

El pasado ya no existe,
Y tú controlas el presente;

Eres más de lo que piensas,
Eres la fuerza de nuestra gente.

Tu poder está por dentro,
Y es más grande que el dolor;

Tu poder está en tu mente,
Y lo que está en tu Corazón.

Tú escribes tu futuro,
Que hoy parece un mar sin agua;

Poco a poco se va llenando,
Y va aliviando esa alma.

Y cuando todo parezca imposible,
Y quieras rendirte y bajar tu cabeza . . . .

Recuerda, tu sacrificio de hoy en día,
Mañana será tu recompensa.

César E. Becerra

Más Allá Del Horizonte

Ya llegamos al final pero el camino solo empieza;

Con el tiempo has crecido a ser una persona con nobleza.

Lo realmente importante no se aprende en una clase;

Se aprende con las lecciones y las decisiones que uno hace.

Su camino fue más largo y también mucho más duro;

Pero el gozo de su logro lo hará sentirse más seguro.

Tenga seguridad que en cada caída existe la fuerza para levantar;

También que con la vida, cada persona va a cambiar.

Hay que luchar para ser la persona que siempre has querido ser;

Tiene que ser la respuesta a las preguntas que nadie quiere hacer.

El futuro será suyo pero hay que brincar cada barrera;

Lo crucial no es ser primero, solo terminar esa carrera.

Enfóquese en su presente porque el pasado ya se ha ido;

Más allá del horizonte se encuentra el camino a su destino.

Más allá del horizonte hay montañas que escalar;

Aunque el destino ya este escrito, el camino hay que buscar.

No tenga miedo a tener éxito y no le tema al fracaso;

Hasta la más larga jornada empieza con un solo paso.

De las gracias por lo que tiene y no se queje por lo que se le niega;

Tiene la oportunidad de alcanzar un sueño . . . para algunos nunca llega.

El propósito de la vida

es un enigma sin respuesta;

Apreciar cada momento

Es realmente lo que cuenta.

Busquen siempre ese valor para soñar

Chapter 12

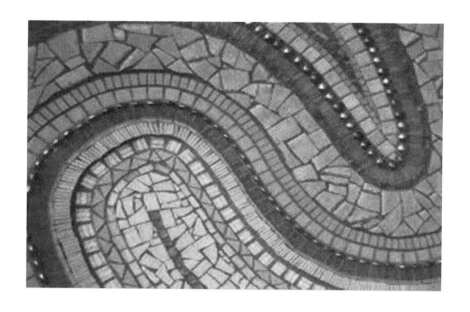

Last Words

The Choice

There's a pain that lives within me,
A pain that is now hard to conceal;

It's a pain that resides next to fear,
Yet the truth it can't reveal.

I fear the choices that we are making,
Choices made with a free will;

Some choose love, some choose to hate,
It seems the end is all too near.

Some say that love, it reigns eternal,
And that it is perhaps all that we need;

But there is hate, hate is a virus,
It spreads throughout and makes you weak.

The choice is yours; it's your decision,
Spread love or apathy.

It's that choice that haunts me daily,
And at night, keeps me from sleep.

César E. Becerra

Unos viven en el pasado

Otros en el presente

El límite de mi vida

Está en la imaginación en mi mente.

Se Busca

Se busca un asesino que ha matado por muchos años.
Ha matado a niños, hombres, mujeres y tirados los ha dejado.

No le han hecho ningún mal pero aún les tiene un temor grande,
No sabía lo que sentían porque nunca tuvo hambre.

Todas sus víctimas eran inocentes, gente como tú o yo,
Gente que ya no tiene futuro, estaba cerca y se escapó.

Todos tenían humildes sueños, y esperanza para mañana;
Que destino les toco, de su vida no quedó nada.

Solo quedan los recuerdos, y el eco de sus llantos;
Cada día mueren más, quien le irá a poner un alto.

Dicen que se busca el asesino pero para mí es algo obvio,
Sigue en el mismo lugar de siempre, manifestando siempre el odio.

Si de veras quieren encontrarlo les sugiero que abran los ojos,
Miren bien lo que se sufre, los que triunfan son muy pocos.

Les revelo el asesino más grande en mi vida,
Tanto dolor y tragedia, ha roto tantas familias.

Lo maldigo desde niño porque me quito mi identidad,
Finalmente la he encontrado y he escrito mi verdad.

Les revelo otra verdad en lágrimas porque de mi sonrisa nada queda;
El asesino más grande en mi vida ha sido y seguirá siendo nuestra frontera.

La unidad es y siempre será nuestra fuerza

Dear Joe,

I write this letter as a citizen of the world and out of great love for our nation; my hope is still alive and well although I'm close to exasperation. I also write in a state of mourning because the values I love are slowly dying. I respect your right to an opinion and the ability to voice it, but I can't condone your lying. The flagrant abuse of power makes me fearful of where we are going. Under your "heroic leadership", a culture of fear is slowly growing. I'm so sick of your "border battle", your media sound bites and blatant racism; for me the issue is much simpler; humanity will always come before patriotism. I took the time to get to know you by doing some research about your life. Your life definitely hasn't been easy and when I think of your lack of compassion I can only wonder why. Was your family part of the original settlers or did they come from overseas? I wonder how much they sacrificed to make sure you could succeed. You're from a family of immigrants, so are you not a true "American"? Do you understand imperialism? Two hundred years ago, in this land you would be Mexican. What was the name of the ship that they came over on? Perhaps it was the famous Mayflower? Who the hell defined "American" and tell me how they got that power? I wonder what their reasons were for leaving their home, have you ever asked them "why"?

César E. Becerra

How were they treated when they got here, ask them how it feels to cry? The later generations came on ships, arriving on Ellis Island to open ports. But what if the ports were closed, what if we had shut all the doors? Do you think they would turn around and go back or would they try everything to stay? Would they give up their dream that easily or do you think they'd find a way? Let me ask you a few more questions and you can tell me what you would do. What would you do if you lived in a country where corruption reigned supreme? Please imagine working a lifetime and barely having the resources to meet your daily needs. When opportunity and hope has all but perished do you think crossing a line would be a risk worth taking? Tell me if you were in that predicament would you wait for change to come or would you do anything to make it? Do you remember the great wars or how we got through the depression? We don't have to look that far, how do we get through each recession? In many of our battles, who were the first soldiers deployed? When our work force was overseas fighting, what country's labor did we exploit? Not all soldiers were pale in color many brown faces were present. Have you ever given that one thought? Perhaps it just was not worth a second. Do you ever look at the image in the mirror and wonder what you have become: A manifestation of hate and anger; your ancestors must be very proud. Have you ever stopped to look, at the pain that's on their face? Better yet, answer this question: What would I do in their place?

The Long and Winding Road

Perhaps the essence of life is confusion
And our reason for living we will never see.
Maybe the best approach to life
Is not to question but to believe.
I have been on a road and journey
From the moment of my birth.
The world is a giant classroom
And our mission is to learn.
I have learned so many lessons,
They are difficult to recall.
Every one of those lessons have shaped me
Into the person I have become.
I have become a person of courage
Yet one who is not afraid to cry.
When life seems overwhelming
You must take everything in stride.
I will continue on this long and winding road
"Live and learn" will be my creed.
I will finish my life's journey;
Wherever that winding road may lead.

César E. Becerra

Last Words

This is for the seeds that will never get to grow.

This is for the future that we will never know.

This is for our people that were just too blind to see.

This is for potential and all the things I'll never be.

My song is for the answers to the questions they never ask.

And for all those lonely shadows that hide behind a mask.

My song is for all people who never learned to believe

And for those who are trying to find the courage to succeed.

These words are for the struggle and eternal sacrifice.

Mortal beings soon disappear but strong words will never die.

These words I write in agony and incredible lament.

You had an opportunity; and now you don't know where it went.

Dios Mío,

Gracias por darme vida un día más y por permitirme disfrutar de los regalos que me has dado. Me siento bendecido por que siempre me perdonas por todas mis debilidades como persona. Has hecho tanto por mí y las bendiciones continúan. Perdóname por todo lo que he hecho este día que no fue de tu agrado. Por favor perdóname y mantenme libre de peligro y daño. Ayúdame para empezar mi mañana con un nuevo comportamiento y con mucha gratitud. Ayúdame a aprovechar el nuevo día a lo máximo y a limpiar mi mente para poder oír tu voz cuando me quieras hablar. Ayúdame también a abrir mi mente para poder aceptar las cosas que son difíciles de aceptar. No me permitas perder sueño sobre las cosas que no controlo. Ayúdame a levantarme cuando he caído. Cuando no rece mis oraciones por favor escucha a mi Corazón. Te pido que me continúes bendiciendo para poder ser una bendición para mis semejantes. Ayúdame a ser fuerte para tener el valor para ayudar a los que están débiles. Mantenme motivado para poder encontrar las palabras que motiven a los que las necesiten. Te pido por todos aquellos que estén perdidos y que no puedan encontrar su camino. Te pido también por aquellos que son juzgados por los demás. Te pido por todos los que aún no te conocen. Finalmente, pido por todos los que no creen en el poder del amor. Dios mío: te quiero y te necesito. Te ruego que busques y encuentres mi Corazón. Nunca me abandones.

This is my life . . .

The love I found is the most vital
reason for breathing . . .

You give me strength, you're my humility . . .

You are my reason for believing.

You are the Colors On My Canvas...
The End... is only

The Beginning

About the Author

César E. Becerra is proud to call himself a continental American of Mexican Heritage. As the oldest of three children and raised in a modest family in the agricultural heart of Central California, he realized at an early age that he had a responsibility to lead and provide a good example for his siblings. He is grateful for the many values instilled in him by his parents that have allowed him to define true success and have the courage to strive for it. César was the first in his family to attend and graduate from a university and chose to pursue a career in education and counseling as a way of continuing to lead and provide examples for the future leaders of our communities. César is passionate about teaching and learning and understands that there are lessons to be learned from our successes and our failures. He currently resides in the state of Arizona with his wife and two sons where he continues to work diligently at the ever needed task of inspiring young minds and instilling hope in the hearts of those who need it. César is a true advocate for students and has an unyielding belief in the power of the human spirit.